Shintō:
The Gospel's Gate

Brian T. McGregor

Shintō: the Gospel's Gate

Cover Photo Credit: Brian T. McGregor. August 25, 2017
Konoshima Jinja, Kyoto.
The torii pictured leads to a pond and the three-legged torii.

Part 1 was previously published as On Ancient Paths: From the Garden to the Grave by Brian T. McGregor. Printed through Create Space in 2016.

Unless otherwise indicated, all Scripture quotations are from The ESV® Bible (the Holy Bible, English Standard Version®), copyright © 2001 by Crossway, a publishing ministry of Good News Publishers. Used by Permission. All Rights reserved.

Scripture quotations marked HCSB are taken from the Holman Christian Standard Bible, Copyright 1999, 2000, 2002, 2003, 2009 by Holman Bible Publishers. Used by permission. Holman Christian Standard Bible, Holman CSB, and HCSB are federally registered trademarks of Holman Bible Publishers.

Scripture quotations marked (LEB) are from the Lexham English Bible. Copyright 2013 Lexham Press. Lexham Press is a registered trademark of Faithlife Corporation.

Copyright © 2019 Brian McGregor
All rights reserved.
ISBN-13: 9781793085597

TABLE OF CONTENTS

	Acknowledgments	i
	Part 1: From the Garden to the Grave	**1**
	Preface	3
1	Biblical Worldview	5
2	Shintō Worldview	17
3	Evaluation	23
4	Touchpoint: Creator	25
5	Touchpoint: Impurity	33
6	Psalm 51	37
7	Psalm 51: Hebrew Words	41
8	Diagnosing Sin	49
9	Conclusion Part 1	57
	Part 2: From Death to Life	**59**
10	Crisis and Resolution	61
11	Jōtei Revisited	65
12	Psalm 51 part 2	73
13	Yom Kippur	79
14	Yom Kippur: Word Study	85
15	Yom Kippur: Scapegoat	95
16	Oharai	101
17	Shintō Sacrifice	111
18	Typology	119
19	Hebrews	133
20	Analogy and Application	143
21	Answering the Challenge	153
22	Salvation Triad	159
23	Conclusion	165
	Appendix 1: Beyond Japan	167
	Appendix 2 Identifying Shame	171

Appendix 3 Shame Drama	181
Foreign Words Lexicon	183
Works Cited	189
Works Consulted	195
Index of Graphs, and Tables	198
About the Author	199

ACKNOWLEDGMENTS

In some ways, I began writing Shintō: the Gospel's Gate in 2012 with "The Shame Drama: The Fall" (see appendix 2 and 3). In other ways I did not begin writing it until 2015. I published On Ancient Paths: From the Garden to the Grave in 2016 because I had a pressing conviction that being able to explain sin to the Japanese would make a difference for some Japanese seekers. I could not hold onto the Story of Tsumi and the Shame Triad while I tried to finish the redemptive analogy.

It was almost two and a half years of additional research to try and iron out the theology behind the analogy that I had identified during my last semester of MDiv study at Columbia International University. I knew that it would cause major problems if I was not able to explain the biblical background for the analogy.

During that time, I received encouragement from several people who work in the area of Japanese evangelism and intercultural studies. Among these are Dr. Timothy Boyle, Dr. David Cashin, Professor Anne Crescini, Dr. Bill Jones, Dr. Daniel Kikawa, Dr. Samuel Lee, and Dr. Ezekiel Xu.

I want to particularly thank Dr. Boyle for pointing out a mistake in my spelling of yūrei. I had written it with a short u, resulting in the kanji for 'cold oil'. Dr. Boyle also suggested a change in the spelling of 上帝 Jyōtei to 上帝 Jōtei since it would be more natural for English speakers to pronounce it correctly.

Meeting Dr. Boyle and developing the Story of Tsumi would not have been possible without the support of Second Level Ministry. A special thankyou to Mayumi Pohl and everyone else I worked with during two semesters as an intern.

Lastly, I want to thank my wife, Yan Wang, who has been a sounding board and an encouragement as I sorted through difficult theology.

PART 1: FROM THE GARDEN TO THE GRAVE

"By the sweat of your face you shall eat bread, till you return to the ground, for out of it you were taken; for you are dust, and to dust you shall return."
---- Genesis 3:19 (ESV)

Shintō: the Gospel's Gate

Preface

One problem with communicating the Gospel to the Japanese people is that Western theology was developed in a Latin and Greek speaking, guilt-based culture. This has two results: first, the terminology that was developed uses the Greek words, making it difficult for those who do not know Greek to understand what is being discussed; and second, much of the theology is centered on a legal understanding of the Bible's message.

The first issue is easily dealt with by giving a quick translation and an introduction to the issues covered by the category. For example, *theology* is the combination of two Greek words. *Theo* was the word adapted to mean 'god', and *ology* means 'study of'. So, theology is 'the study of god'. But being in a Western framework the study of god primarily is concerned with things that are relevant to a guilt-based culture.

The Doctrine of Salvation, Propitiation, Sanctification, Hamartiology, etc. became the categories that the Western half of the Roman Empire placed their emphasis on. Being able to explain the content of these doctrines (right teachings) was critically important in the Early Church period as people tried to understand just what the implications of the Gospel *were*. So, Early Church history is full of conflict as theologians sought to protect the Church from false teachers and their false teachings.

Unfortunately, one aspect of the consequence of this history is that many times the Western Church became so focused on defining theological truth that they lost the relationship of the Gospel to the heart of the believer.

Social scientists who study culture have developed three labels to categorize how cultures function. Shame-based cultures are those primarily concerned with maintaining social status. Fear-based cultures are primarily concerned with the spiritual forces that inhabit the unseen world. Guilt-based cultures are primarily concerned with maintaining innocence.

With Western theology having been developed almost exclusively in a guilt-based context, Westerners have great difficulty in relating the Bible to shame-based and fear-based cultures. There has been a marked increase in efforts by ministry workers to communicate the Gospel in a way that connects to these other two cultural systems.

Those from shame-based and fear-based cultures have been developing their own way of discussing and developing the core issues of the Bible, but Westerners have generally remained ignorant or unable to let go of their own categories to engage in dialogue with those outside of the guilt-based narrative.

This book is an attempt to add to this cross-cultural work of taking the Gospel out of the prison of guilt-based theology. It will try to present the Gospel in a way that all cultures may more easily appreciate what El Shaddai revealed through Scripture.

This exploration of how the Scriptural framework of sin can be related to the Shintō worldview resists all attempts to put it into a linear format. As a result, there is a cyclical structure to develop the different aspects of this discussion. It may seem to move from one topic to another without clear reasoning to the shift. Please keep in mind that this is meant to be an introduction to a way to communicate the Gospel to the Japanese Shintō worldview, not a theology.

There are many things that could be developed further, but the focus here is to examine the aspects of the story in Scripture in a way that is accessible to non-academics. Different parts of the discussion will have a more academic feel to it, but hopefully everyone will be able to follow the thought and progression without needing specialized theological training.

Names of God

It is necessary at the beginning of this book to discuss the use of names for God. I am particular about how to address the God of Abraham, Isaac, and Jacob. The word "god" is actually a Germanic word referring to beings of great power, like the Greek gods, the Irish Fae, the Hebrew El, and the Japanese Kami. I find it better to use the proper names for the God of

Shintō: the Gospel's Gate

Scripture, the Hebrew designates Yahweh (YHWH) or El Shaddai, the divine title distinctive to the God of the patriarchs (Ex 6:3).[1]

There is strong evidence that YHWH did not only reveal himself to the Hebrews, but to most people groups. *Eternity in Their Hearts* by Don Richardson[2] is the best resource I am aware of for the discussion of this phenomenon.

Currently in Japan, the word used for YHWH is a Western missionary construct, 神様 Kami-Sama[3] which has a very short history and causes confusion to Japanese who have not been instructed in its use. Being of Irish descent, I can only imagine that 神様 Kami-Sama poses the same problems that would exist if the original missionaries to Ireland had decided to use the term "Chief of the Fae" to describe YHWH, making Him just another spiritual being among many.

One option to better communicate the identity of the Creator to the Japanese people is to use the Hebrew terms or linguistically native terms, such as 天之御中主の神 Amenominakanushi no Kami. In the video *God's Fingerprints in Japan*[4] research is presented that the proper Japanese name for the Creator God is Amenominakanushi あめのみなきぬし – 天之御中主. *God's Fingerprints* details that 天之御中主 Amenominakanushi can be traced back to before the writing of the *Kojiki* around 700 AD. Despite this history, Aloha Ke Akua points out that 天之御中主 is not well known in Japan.

In relation to the authenticity of 天之御中主の神 Amenominakanushi,

> We can with some degree of probability conclude that Ame-no-Minakanushi-

---

[1] K. A. Mathews, *Genesis 11:27–50:26 vol. 1B* (Nashville: Broadman & Holman Publishers, 2005), 907.

[2] Don Richardson, *Eternity in Their Hearts, third edition* (Bethany House Publishers, 2008).

[3] Based on personal conversations with professors, missionaries and Japanese Christians. I have also heard the explanation that *Kami-Sama* originally referred to objects of worship; in this case *Kami-Sama* would be a synonym for 'idol.' *Kami-Sama* does not appear in the reference books that I have access to, so its origin is unknown to me.

[4] Daniel Kikawa, *God's Fingerprints in Japan Vol 1&2* (Aloha Ke Akua Ministries, 2008. DVD).

no-Kami [The Divine Lord of the Very Center of Heaven] is the God of the so-called primitive monotheism indigenous to the soil of Japan and we find little or no trace of importation from China of such monotheism.[5]

In light of the apparent obscurity of 天之御中主 Amenominakanushi in the Japanese mind, there is another option which satisfies this author's desire of a native term for YHWH that reflects Japanese cultural roots.

The Chinese designate is 上帝 ShangDi, which can be traced back to 2500 B.C. and translates as Emperor of Heaven, as demonstrated by C. H. Kang[6] and is currently used in Chinese translations of Scripture, and phonetically sounds like Shaddai (Gen. 17:1). 上帝 is employed by the Japanese language with the pronunciation Jōtei じょうてい.[7] Yet another option is 天帝 てんてい tentei, which is more clearly 'Heavenly Emperor'.

For this book, I will use 上帝 as Jōtei because: it traces back to Chinese and Japanese history; it helps avoid the confusion that 神様 Kami-Sama causes; and it helps establish the link that the God of Abraham, Isaac, and Jacob is not a Western deity.

---

[5] Katao Genchi, *Study of Shintō: the Religion of the Japanese Nation* (Tōkyō: The Zaidan-Hōjin-Meiji-Seitoku-Kinen-Gakkai, 1926), 66.

[6] C. H. Kang, *Discovery of Genesis in the Chinese Language* (St. Louis: Concordia Publishing House, 1979), 2, 20.

[7] http://nihongo.monash.edu/cgi-bin/wwwjdic?1C search jyoutei result: (1) Shangdi (creator deity in Chinese folk religion); (2) God (in Christianity). Accessed 10-21-15.

Chapter 1 Biblical Worldview

A worldview answers four broad questions. The first three are origin, purpose, and crisis. Where did the world come from? What is the purpose of human life? What went wrong? My framework for answering these questions in the Christian worldview is laid out in this chapter. Chapter 2 will introduce the Shintō worldview as I understand it.

In some ways a worldview can be understood as the metanarrative, the overriding story which helps us make sense out of the world. And Scripture is one great piece of literature, from the opening lines of Genesis to the closing word of Revelation. There are many types of literature within this great work – prophecy, history, tragedy, poetry, letters, wisdom, and mourning. The beginning of a story sets the narrative in history, introduces the main characters, and presents the crisis.

The Gospels answer the fourth worldview question, the resolution to the crisis. There are many references in the Gospel to the Old Testament prophets, history, and poetry. Too often, we begin telling the story of Scripture to outsiders at the Gospels, which are the climax of the story of Scripture.

But what if we began telling the story at the beginning?

The story of Scripture begins with only one character: 上帝 Jōtei, God, El Shaddai, the Creator. There is no explanation for the origin of 上帝 Jōtei, He is the uncaused caused, the originator. As 上帝 Jōtei creates, the setting is narrowed until we are looking at one man in a garden. 上帝 Jōtei calls this man His son and they walk together without separation. But then there is the crisis. The Serpent comes into the Garden and causes the man to be relationally separated from his father. The man is expelled from his perfect home and 上帝 Jōtei promises to one day overcome the Serpent.

What are the most important points of this way of looking at the story of

Scripture?

First, the main character of Scripture is 上帝 Jōtei, not humanity.

Second, Scripture tells a story of a relationship. When 上帝 Jōtei told Adam not to eat from the Tree of the Knowledge of Good and Evil, it was a relational command, not a law. Condemning one person to death because of one piece of fruit is incredibly harsh, condemning an entire race – millions of millions of people – because of one piece of fruit is simply unimaginably cruel. There has to be something more to the story than breaking a household rule.

Third, the crisis of Scripture is the separation between 上帝 Jōtei and mankind because of man's rebellion. This crisis arose because 上帝 Jōtei's enemy came into the garden and challenged 上帝 Jōtei's honor. The man listened and rebelled. 上帝 Jōtei is not an evil, capricious Creator, but someone who cares deeply for the wellbeing of his creation and his own reputation – his honor.

Now it is a question of how 上帝 Jōtei will answer the enemy's challenge. One of the questions a story must answer is, "Why do the characters do what they do?" Enlightenment Christianity provides a motivation of love for why Jesus is willing to die in our place. For many people, however, this is simply not a believable explanation. For instance, I had a conversation with a Wiccan[1] and she asked, "If God loves me so much, why won't he just let me into heaven regardless of what I believe?" Others object that love is not a strong enough motivation, and yet others will object that there is no honor in Jesus' death on the cross. The next few sections will help us answer that objection.

Crisis

With the story properly framed around the 上帝 Jōtei, we need to move into the plot of the story. Let us look at the Genesis account of the creation and rebellion of humanity.

Genesis 3 tells us how mankind was the pinnacle of 上帝 Jōtei's creation. Adam was honored above all of creation:

---

[1] a type of witch who emphasizes feminine energy and elemental power.

上帝 Jōtei had formed his body by hand, breathed into his mouth directly, placed him in a home specially made for him, named the man His son, gave him work, provided every type of plant for food, created a special help-mate for him, gave him authority over all life on Earth, and walked with him in the cool of the evening.[2]

To simplify the account, there are only two characters present in the Garden narrative: 上帝 Jōtei and humanity. There was just one thing that 上帝 Jōtei held back: the man was not to eat from the Tree of the Knowledge of Good and Evil. 上帝 Jōtei has made a claim to honor, "I am your Creator and deserve to be honored as your father, obey my command."

But then one day, the Serpent came into the Garden, approached the man, and asked, "Did 上帝 Jōtei say …?"

Through his question, the Serpent challenges 上帝 Jōtei's character and claim to honor with the accusation, "上帝 Jōtei does not deserve your loyalty. He is keeping the very best from you."

The man, soon to be named Adam, is at this point in an untested state. He only knows 上帝 Jōtei's best – there was no illness, no danger from animals or weather, and no shame. This is a point of high court drama, but those familiar with the story lose the sense of anticipation.

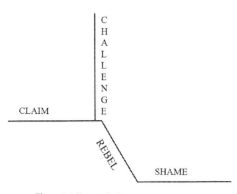

Figure 1.1 Honor Challenge

Adam eats the fruit of the Tree of the Knowledge of Good and Evil and his eyes are immediately opened. He realizes he is naked, sews fig-leaves together for clothing, and hides when he hears 上帝 Jōtei walking in the Garden. When 上帝 Jōtei finds the man, the main dialogue can be summarized as "This is your fault, 上帝 Jōtei!"

Adam had a claim to honor as 上帝 Jōtei's son, but after listening to the accusation of the Serpent, he rebelled

---

[2] Jason Georges, In the Beginning . . . Honor, http://honorshame.com/beginning-honor/ posted 9-24-14, last accessed 1-6-16.
My list is a summary of Jason George's article.

and lost that honored position. No longer was the garden his home. No longer would the land simply produce food for him. No longer were the animals and plants subject to him. No longer did he find joy in his work. No longer was he without shame.

上帝 Jōtei's honor was also damaged by Adam's rebellion; his intimate fellowship with Adam had been lost. 上帝 Jōtei is and was the creator of the world, both physical and spiritual. He had honor before He began creation from, through, and by His very being (Col. 1:16). This intrinsic honor did not change, but His relational honor with humanity was damaged.

Taking a step back, the reader may object that I am excluding Eve from this narrative overview. This is true, but I am doing it for the sake of clarity. First, 上帝 Jōtei's command not to eat from the Tree of the Knowledge of Good and Evil was given to the man before the creation of the woman. Second, it was the man's responsibility to teach the woman about 上帝 Jōtei's command; when she misquotes it, we are left to wonder if it was her mistake or if the man had added to 上帝 Jōtei's command. Third, the man was standing with the woman when the Serpent came and spoke with her and she ate from the tree. Fourth, it was not until the man ate from the forbidden fruit that their eyes were opened.

It seems clear in this that the curse of rebellion came into play when the man disobeyed 上帝 Jōtei. It is through the man that the effects of the curse are handed down from generation to generation. During the sentencing, 上帝 Jōtei tells the woman, "Your seed will crush the Serpent's head" (Gen. 3:15, HCSB). This is a curious phrase because throughout Scripture women are spoken of bearing fruit, while men are credited with seed.

For the sake of clarity of the drama, I have chosen to see the man and woman as one entity of humanity. There may be a legal dimension to the narrative, but I think it is better seen as a relational drama. Will the man and woman honor 上帝 Jōtei and obey His command, or will they dishonor Him? Unfortunately for us all, they chose the path of dishonor.

At various times I have wondered just what the Knowledge of Good and Evil was. Did Adam suddenly understand stealing, murder, espionage, war, lying, assault, identity theft, speeding, and so on?

The way the Western Church has told the story, Adam suddenly knew all the moral and criminal law. As such, the Western explanation of sin uses the concept of guilt as a turning point. Certainly, the man was guilty of violating the command given him, but how do we *see* the action of guilt manifest in the narrative? We do not, because guilt is a noun, not a verb.

If guilt is not something that can be pictured, a definition is needed. Guilt arises from violating some internalized value system[3] and the attendant fear of punishment.[4] This is the first issue with using guilt as a synonym for sin. The second issue becomes manifest in cross-cultural communication. If guilt is the result of *violating an internalized law*, then why should people without Mosaic Law feel guilty for violating Scriptural commands?

We have the challenge then of convincing people that they are guilty of breaking 上帝 Jōtei's law.

To say someone is guilty is the same as accusing someone of being a criminal. Even in Western contexts this is extremely offensive, more so in a culture that treats direct confrontation negatively. Kagawa Toyohiko relates the problem in this way,

> "The Japanese have a strong antipathy for the concept of sin . . . . The Japanese, with their aversion to criticism and their unyielding spirit, will not readily recognize the sin in their own soul."[5]

The Villain

Attention needs to be brought to the villain of Scripture. In the Genesis account, he is only identified as the Serpent, but we find out as Scripture progresses that the Serpent is Satan, who in Revelation is described as a Red Dragon. To understand Satan's motives, we need to look at where he came from.

---

[3] Timothy Tennent, *Theology in the Context of World Christianity* (Grand Rapids: Zondervan, 2007), 129.

[4] G. Piers and M. Singer, *Shame and Guilt: A Psychoanalytic and Cultural Study* (New York: Horton, 1953), quoted in Timothy Laniak Shame and Honor in the Book of Esther (Atlanta, Society of Biblical Literature, 1998), 24.

[5] Kagawa Toyohiko, *Christ and Japan, third printing* (New York: Friendship Press, 1934), 44-45.

Shintō: the Gospel's Gate

Scripture gradually develops a robust spirit world occupied by various types of angels. Genesis does not tell us when the angels were created because the Creation account is focused on the physical world, so the spirit world is outside of its narrative. However, Colossians 1:16 and John 1:3 says that all things in heaven and earth were created by and through Christ and nothing came into existence except through Him.

Considering this, the Serpent, also called Satan, was created by 上帝 Jōtei, yet the Genesis account says that 上帝 Jōtei looked at the world and said that it was very good (Gen. 1:31). We are told that 上帝 Jōtei does not lie (Numbers 23:19) and He condemns those who call evil good (Isaiah 5:20).

If 上帝 Jōtei had created Satan as the father of lies (John 8:44), how could He say that everything was good? The only answer that fits the evidence is that Satan was created good, but somewhere between Genesis 1 and 3 he became evil.

This book is not focused on Biblical Demonology, consequently we will not be able to document the precedents for interpreting some of the imagery used to describe Satan's fall in the prophets. As we examine this, keep in mind that the prophets sometimes speak of things with double referents. It is a methodology sometimes referred to as progressive prophecy, where the prophecy has a near fulfillment and a distant fulfillment (such as Isaiah 7:14). This can also be applied to using earthly things to speak of heavenly things. One branch of this is called typology.

There are rules to typological interpretation and there are limitations. Simply explained, 上帝 Jōtei will speak of heavenly things through physical representations as in John 3:12. And these physical examples may be 'sketches and shadows of heavenly things' (Heb. 8:4-5).

Ezekiel, Isaiah, Revelation

Ezekiel 28:1-19 tells about the king of Tyre, but the language cannot be properly applied to a human. Humans are humans and will always be human, yet this passage refers to the King of Tyre as a cherub – an angelic being described as having the face of a man, the body of a lion, and the wings of an eagle. Moving the account out of Hebrew parallelism and focusing on the action, we are told:

Shintō: the Gospel's Gate

> King of Tyre, you were created perfect with the fullness of wisdom and beauty and stood in the Garden of Eden. You were stationed as a guardian cherub, appointed to the holy mountain of 上帝 Jōtei. You were blameless in all your ways until corruption was found in you. Your heart became exalted because of your beauty, for the sake of your glory you corrupted your wisdom. Your heart became full of violent plans and you rebelled. You were expelled in disgrace from my holy mountain. (Ez. 28:1-19, paraphrased)

Another sketch of Satan comes from Isaiah 14 (table 1.1). In context, Isaiah is speaking about the king of Babylon and predicting how he will be removed from power. Isaiah moves from speaking of a human king to language that can only apply to an angelic being. The stars mentioned here are representative of angels (Rev. 12:4) and the clouds refer to the glory of 上帝 Jōtei (Ex. 40:34-35, 1 Kings 8:10-11).

> Isaiah 14:12-14
> How you are fallen from heaven, Day Star, son of the dawn!
> How you are cut down to the ground, you who brought down nations.
> You said in your heart,
> "I will ascend to heaven, above the stars of God.
> I will set my throne above the mountain of assembly . . .
> I will ascend above the highest clouds.
> I will be as the Most High."
> But you are cast down. (paraphrased)
> Table 1.1 Isaiah 14

We can see from these accounts that Satan was created as the highest of the angels as a cherub, the angels that were placed on top of the Ark of the Covenant, and his name was Lucifer. Ezekiel 28:1 tells us that Lucifer was in the Garden of Eden, which probably indicates that he was an eyewitness to the creation of man and 上帝 Jōtei's command not to eat from the Tree of Knowledge.

However, somewhere between Genesis 2 and 3 Lucifer rebelled. He became focused on his own glory and beauty and desired to have more glory, 'you corrupted your wisdom for the sake of your beauty.' In Proverbs 9:10 we are told that the beginning of wisdom is the fear of the Lord, which indicates that Lucifer abandoned the fear of the Lord. He no longer respected 上帝 Jōtei as the Creator and thought he could become greater than 上帝 Jōtei.

At this point Lucifer rebelled and he corrupted his sanctuary. This is an odd terminology unless we consider the Hebrew. Sanctuary in Hebrew is written מִקְדָּשׁ *miqdash* which is constructed by adding the preposition מִ *mi*, which basically means 'place of', to קָדוֹשׁ *qadosh* which means 'holy'.[6] The picture then is that Lucifer corrupted the holy place of his heart, the area that was indwelled with 上帝 Jōtei's glory. Lucifer tried to glorify himself and lost the glory which 上帝 Jōtei had given him.

After rebelling in his heart, Lucifer gathered other angels to his cause and led them in a war against 上帝 Jōtei. Revelation 12:3-4, 7-9 records the event as a great red dragon sweeping one third of the stars from heaven and being thrown to the earth.

Lucifer, now Satan, was expelled from heaven, but not destroyed. He had set out to overthrow 上帝 Jōtei and lost. Revelation 12:12 concludes the scene of Lucifer's rebellion by declaring, "But woe to you, O earth and sea, for the devil has come down to you in great wrath, because he knows that his time is short!" (ESV)

Defeated and exiled, Satan's heart was full of hate. Unable to defeat 上帝 Jōtei, he attacked 上帝 Jōtei's image bearer. Satan had desired 上帝 Jōtei's glory; taking away the glory of man would be the next best thing. Although we are not given any record of an interchange between Satan and 上帝 Jōtei prior to the temptation in the Garden of Eden, we are shown a parallel scene with the book of Job.

Job 1 records that Satan came before 上帝 Jōtei, who asked him, "Have you considered my servant Job?" To this Satan challenged, "He only worships you because you have blessed him." His accusation is that 上帝 Jōtei is not worshiped for who He is but because of what he has done for Job. With 上帝 Jōtei's permission, Satan attacked Job, first taking away all of his physical blessings of wealth and status and then taking away Job's health.

Something similar was happening in the Garden of Eden. Satan desired to prove that 上帝 Jōtei did not deserve the honor he claimed. If 上帝 Jōtei allowed Adam's rebellion to go unpunished, he would be proven as weak. If he destroyed Adam for his rebellion, Satan would succeed in destroying what

---

[6] All Hebrew words and transliterations are taken from L. A. Mitchel *A Student's Vocabulary for Biblical Hebrew and Aramaic* (Grand Rapids: Zondervan, 1984).

上帝 Jōtei loved.

Adam listened, and Satan took Adam's authority over the earth. Sin entered the world, and with it the crisis of Scripture.

Sin

In some ways, if sin is kept in a legal understanding it is easier to deal with it by ignoring or minimizing its presence in our lives. Those who receive infractions, like parking tickets, do not consider themselves criminals. There's a small fine and then it is forgotten about.

For Westerners, sin is often thought of like these infractions – it is a small lie, a little bit of stolen money, a few careless words – "god loves me, so he will ignore it." As Christians, the thought can be contemptuous (hence the lower case "g") – Jesus already paid the penalty, so it does not matter.

Some of us hear the word 'sin' so often that it just becomes an accepted fact. So how do we explain the concept of sin to those who did not grow up with a Judeo-Christian background? How do we convince people that they should be concerned about breaking the Laws of Moses which they have never heard about?

American culture is changing. Europe's massive decline in Christianity suggests that the understanding of the Gospel in a legal context is losing its persuasiveness. The implication for the church is that we need to change how we are discussing the Gospel. It is necessary to realize that as culture changes, the way we present the Gospel must change in order to show its need.

This is nothing new. Paul wrote that he changed how he explained the Gospel according to the culture that he was reaching out to. Among these different cultural groups were Jews, those focused on law, those not focused on law, and the weak (1 Cor. 9:19-22).

One of the plaguing issues in Japanese evangelism is just how to talk about *what* sin is. The kanji used for sin is 罪 *tsumi*, which represents crime. Thus, the kanji for sinner is 罪人 *tsumibito* which means criminal.

For many Japanese, then, being told they are sinners is the same as being told that they are criminals who have committed such severe crimes as to deserve death. But what laws have they broken to become criminals? Even

Shintō: the Gospel's Gate

the average American would object that they have not gone to jail or done any serious crimes. Such a Gospel is irrelevant to them.

Another issue for the Japanese is that such a direct confrontation itself challenges their sense of honor. It is extremely rude in Japan to point your finger at someone, almost like pointing a knife at someone in America. Linguistically, calling someone a criminal is like pointing a knife at their face. An American might consider how angry they would be if a stranger came up to them and started saying, "You're a thief and a murderer! You deserve to die!"

If our Gospel presentations were handled like this in America, how many people would keep listening? Yet, this is an inherent problem in the Japanese translation of the word 'sin'.

Defining Sin

The word translated as sin from the New Testament Greek is ἁμαρτάνω *hamartano*[7] which most people in the Western church would say means "to miss the mark" referring to God's standards as expressed in the Law of Moses.

This definition seems to be inferred back into the Old Testament translations. The usual word translated as sin in the Old Testament is חָטָא *chata* with the primary verse citation being Judges 20:16 "they [the slingers] all hurled stones and hit precisely, without missing."[8]

Apparently, the definition for sin as missing the mark derives from this one verse in the Old Testament, with confirmation drawn from the New Testament.

However, Scripture was written in Hebrew and was understood in a Hebrew cultural context for over one-thousand years prior to the writing of the New Testament in Greek. Therefore, going Greek words to interpret Hebrew meaning is problematic. For a case in point, חָטָא in Judges 20:16

---

[7] https://www.blueletterbible.org/lang/lexicon/lexicon.cfm? Strongs=G264 accessed 12/17/15.

[8] E. Jenni & C. Westermann, *Theological lexicon of the Old Testament* (Peabody: Hendrickson Publishers, 1997), 407.

could be translated with the phrase 'without error' or 'without separation'.

Another issue with defining sin as 'missing the mark' or breaking God's law is that there is a vast amount of time in human history prior to the introduction of Mosaic Law. Israel was enslaved in Egypt for 400 years after the death of Joseph, Jacob's son. If we define sin as breaking 上帝 Jōtei's laws, then how can people living prior to – or without knowledge of – the Mosaic Law be regarded as sinners?

The Judeo-Christian worldview can be summarized: 1) There is a Creator who brought all things into existence. 2) There are spirit beings called angels, some of whom are evil, as well as people in this world. 3) Humanity was created to glorify and serve the Creator. 4) There is suffering because mankind rebelled against the creator and became separated from Him.

The first step of enculturation is to learn about the worldview being addressed; the second is to evaluate that worldview according to Scriptural worldview; and the third is to express the Truth through a relevant framework. Following such a pattern allows us to join with Paul, who wrote, "To those outside the law I became as one outside the law" (1 Cor. 9:21).

We begin this process in the next chapter.

Shintō: the Gospel's Gate

CHAPTER 2 SHINTŌ WORLDVIEW

The Shintō worldview is difficult to explain as an outsider, and no matter what is written there will be those who disagree. One element of difficulty is that, in Japan, Shintō is often considered a way of living life, rather than a religion. A full introduction to Shintō is impossible in this work, but a general overview and explanation is necessary for those readers who are not familiar with the beliefs and practices of this core expression of Japanese spirituality.

In the broad categorization, Shintō is a form of animism, which holds that spiritual essence is present within all things and people can relate to the spiritual essence with proper ritual.[1] There is no independent creator explicitly perceived in the Shintō worldview. Rather, the universe, and everything in it – natural and supernatural, living and inanimate – is an expression of divine spirit.[2] This includes the kami, which are most closely related with 結び *musubi*, creative energy, as particular aspects of the life principle that permeates all existence.[3]

The universe is progressing from chaos to order, from the confusion of contradictions to a state of harmony, purity, and unity.[4] Such progression could be expressed as the process by which 結び *musubi* is seeking to purify

---

[1] Philip M. Steyne, *Gods of Power* (Columbia: Impact International Foundation, 2005), 34, 38.

[2] J. W. T. Mason, *Meaning of Shintō* (New York: E. P. Dutton and Co., 1935), 44.

[3] James W. Boyd and Ron G. Williams, "Artful Means: An Aesthetic View of Shintō Purification Rituals" *Journal of Ritual Studies* 13, no. 1 (1999): 37-52. *ATLA Religion Database with ATLASerials*, EBSCOhost (accessed Marc 2, 2016), 38.

[4] Sokyo Ono, *Shintō the Kami Way* (Vermont: Charles E. Tuttle Company, 1962), 102.

itself by rightful self-development.[5] This self-development is disrupted by pollution or 穢れ *kegare*[6] which is brought about through actions or conditions called 罪 *tsumi*.

罪 *tsumi* is fundamentally related to death and involves obstructions or distortions of the unfolding creative process of 結び *musubi*; 罪 *Tsumi* includes actions and events for which human beings are morally responsible.[7] George Sansom writes,

> Notice that drawing blood is polluting. 穢 *kega*, which means a wound, was the original word for defilement and in modern language *kegare*, *kegare-ru*, and *kegasu* are used for the words "stain," "to be stained," and "to stain."[8]

Thus, good is understood as pure and clean, while evil is understood as something dirty (impure) or corrupted or brings injury to another.[9] Anything that disturbs the social order . . . and the peaceful development of this world of kami is evil.[10]

A simple list of actions that disrupt community order could be: greed, spreading rumors, stealing, having sex with someone else's spouse, murder, and dishonoring the family.

Government is also part of the social order, so behaviors that are encouraged to maintain national unity could be listed as: celebrate the festivals for the kami and the Emperor; speak the Emperor's name with

---

[5] J. W. T. Mason, *Meaning of Shintō*, 93.

[6] Hoshino Eiki, *Kodansha Encyclopedia of Japan vol 4* (New York: Kodansha International, 1983), 186.

[7] James W. Boyd and Ron G. Williams, "Japanese Shintō: An Interpretation of Priestly Perspective" *Philosophy East & West*. Jan2005, Vol. 55 Issue 1, p33-63. 31p. Accessed from Academic Search Premier 12-22-15. 36.

[8] George Sansom, *A History of Japan vol. 1* (Stanford: Stanford University Press, 1958), 31.

[9] *Japan Illustrated Encyclopedia vol. 1* (New York: Kodansha America, 1993), 767.

[10] Sokyo Ono, *Shintō: The Kami Way* (Vermont: Charles E. Tuttle Company, 1962), 106.

reverence; only serve the Emperor and his officials; there is only one Emperor of Japan.

Origin of *Kegare* 穢れ

If the problem with the world's development is 穢れ *kegare*, two questions to ask are, 'Where does 穢れ *kegare* originate from?' and 'What causes 穢れ *kegare*?'

In the Kojiki, the first account of impurity being brought into the world occurs when the female generative spirit, Izanami, is killed while giving birth to the fire-spirit, Kagutsuchi. Kagutsuchi is described as a serpent, and Izanagi cursed him for killing Izanami before killing him. Kagutsuchi's body then gave birth to innumerable other, lesser, fire spirits.[11]

After some time of mourning, Izanagi traveled to the underworld, the Land of Yomi, and found Izanami had already begun to decay. Upon returning to the land of the living, Izanagi purified himself. It is during this process of purification that Amaterasu, the sun kami, Tsukuyomi, the moon kami, and Suzano-o, the storm kami, were spontaneously produced. Following this, there was conflict between Amaterasu and Suzano-o, which led to Amaterasu hiding in a cave.

From these two accounts Shintō labels two types of *tsumi* as heavenly (*amatsu*) *tsumi* and earthly (*kunitsu*) *tsumi*.[12] Earthly tsumi: Destroying divisions between fields; Double planting of seeds; Driving stakes into mud to cause injury; Spreading excrement over doors; Injuring the skin to cause blood to run; Desecrating a corpse. Heavenly tsumi: Skin irregularities in color, rashes, and warts; Sex with animals; Incest; Uncleanness by lightning; Uncleanness by insects; Different sorts of incantation, witchcraft, curse, and divination.[13]

---

[11] My summary from O. Yasumaro, *Tales from Ancient Japan, or the Kojiki by Yaichiro Isobe* (Tokyo: San Koku Sha, 1929).

[12] Genchi Kato, *A Study of Shintō*, 115.

[13] Correlated from Genchi Katao, *A Study of Shintō*, 112-113, and *Japan Illustrated Encyclopedia vol. 1*).

Shintō: the Gospel's Gate

The Shintō worldview can be expressed as in figure 2.1. 結び *Musubi* is manifesting as 神 *kami*; the 神 *kami* eventually return to 結び *musubi*; the 神 *kami* are impure; and the progression of time is marked by a changing ratio of purity and impurity, although the current measure is unknown.

There is no sense of heaven or hell, or any means by which personality

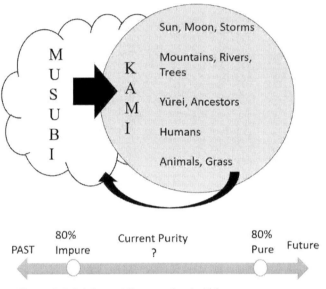

Figure 2.1 Origin and Progression in Shinto

may be retained once the energy of the 神 *kami* returns to 結び *musubi*. Without any sense of heaven, the answer for what happens after we die is that we cease to exist. Those who have become famous live on in the memories of the people and by the faithfulness of those who offer sacrifices for the dead. Because the Shintō worldview includes ghosts, there is the possibility that one will become a ghost suffering whatever torment ghosts are subject to. The world will continue in an endless cycle of death, birth, duty, impurity, and suffering.

Naming the Shintō Worldview

Placing the Shintō worldview into Western philosophical categories seems like a necessary step for Western readers. Normally, Shintō is labeled as

20

either pantheistic or polytheistic. However, these descriptions fail to match the elements assembled in this research. Shintō provides a separate challenge here because of just how unique this worldview is. To describe it, this author has made a new word drawing on Greek labels.

The first part is derived from *panentheism*, all-in-god, which states that god is a finite, changing director of world affairs who works in cooperation with the world in order to achieve greater perfection in his nature.[14] God cannot destroy evil, he must simply work with it and try to overcome it … no final victory over evil is possible.[15]

The second element in the label derives from *polytheism* which holds that there are many gods, each with their own area of control. As noted above, everything is 神 kami – from the sun and moon to the blades of grass, including people.

The third element in the label is *pneumism*, in place of theism. An immediate problem with using the term *theism*, is that it points toward a god, who created and is personally involved in the development of the world, but translating 神 kami as 'god' is perhaps the most inappropriate translation.[16] There is no sense in Shintō that 結び musubi is aware of itself or is participating in the development of the world.[17]

For Shintō, there are many spirits yet none of the spirits are portrayed as a creator or a ruler over all the spirits or the earth. Some kami are more important in Shintō cosmology, such as Amaterasu the Sun Kami. Amaterasu did not create the sun, nor does she rule the sun. She is the spirit of the sun, the sun itself is her body. To be clear, Amaterasu is the 神 kami of the sun: her mind can be known through proper ritual and her body is seen in the sky.

Combining the terms listed above produces *panenpolypneumism*. 結び

---

[14] Norman L. Geisler and William D. Watkins, *Worlds Apart: A Handbook on Worldviews; second edition* (Eugene: Wipf and Stock Publishers, 2003), 107-108.

[15] ibid. 114-5

[16] Stuart D. B. Picken, *Historical Dictionary of Shintō: Historical Dictionaries of Religions, Philosophies, and Movements no. 38* (Lanham: Scarecrow Press, 2002), 105.

[17] J. W. T. Mason, *Meaning of Shintō*, 44.

Shintō: the Gospel's Gate

musubi spontaneously generates 神 *kami* and does not have any personality or will, so it cannot interact with or be known by the 神 *kami* or the natural world. The natural world is the physical representation of many spirits, or 神 *kami*, all of which are in process.

As each of these 神 *kami* progress the result should be positive growth. But 神 *kami* make mistakes called 罪 *tsumi* resulting in 穢れ *kegare* which must be purified. Not all of these 神 *kami* have physical bodies, and some manifest as 幽霊 *Yūrei* (angry ghosts) or the spirits of ancestors. All of these spirits are able to interact with the physical realm and must be enticed or appeased for the welfare of people. The levels of spirits and nature are expressed in figure 2.2.

By implication, a rough analogy would be: water is taken from the ocean (結び *musubi*), frozen, then carved into a sculpture (神 *kami*); while the sculpture exists, it gives pleasure to those around it; when the ice sculpture melts, the water returns to the ocean; eventually a new mix of water is reintroduced as a new sculpture. This process continues without end and without any moral judgment of the ocean upon the actions of the ice sculpture. There can be no moral judgment because the ice sculpture ceases to be an individual entity and returns to impersonal water.

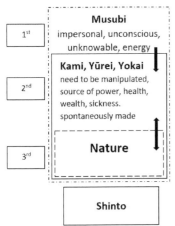

Figure 2.2 Shintō Levels

CHAPTER 3 EVALUATION

To begin this discussion, let the author state that the Japanese are a beautiful, noble people, doing their best to find a way out of this world of suffering. Shintō, as the backbone of Japanese culture, is just as beautiful with its awareness of the mystery of nature and the certainty that there is something more to this world than flesh and bone.

Like all countries and people groups, there are periods of Japanese history that are difficult and even terribly painful to deal with. It is a tragedy that many missionaries and churches have addressed Japan as though the culture itself is bad and there is something wrong with the Japanese being Japanese.

This is an attitude that has been faced by many cultures when the Western nations encountered them. It is beyond terrible the way that the European Empires used Christianity as a tool to expand their control; even more reprehensible is when Christians tell people that their very culture is shameful. This type of attitude is not limited to Europe, as the United States of America has many such stains in our history.

Although this is only in written form and I am not an important person, I humbly ask for forgiveness. I do not ask on behalf of the Western nations, but on behalf of Christ for the way the Western Church twisted and misused Scripture for personal gain. In the zeal to bring Good News to new people groups, such attitudes and behaviors smeared and defiled the very image of the One who commissioned the mission.

Shintō has shown an intuitive grasp that there is more to this world than what can be seen or measured. There is a very rich spirit-world and a knowledge that the world had to emerge from something. For Shintō this point of emergence is the unknowable, unseen, ever-present force of 結び *musubi*. As an energy source without personality, 結び *musubi* cannot be known, and it has no directive power in the events of the world.

However, Shintō recognizes the need for direction in the world – there must be a personality or mind that directs the natural order of life, death, reproduction, growth, and seasons. For this process Shintō turns to the High Kami such as Amaterasu, Suzano-o, and Tsukuyomi. Every critical life system is directed by a Kami which directs lesser kami. For instance, there is a Kami of the Harvest who directs or oversees the kami of rice, buckwheat, sweet potatoes and so forth. These kami representing a particular crop oversee or direct the individual kami expressed by the individual plants.

Shintō recognizes there is a problem: when one of the kami – great or small, human or elemental, plant or animal – strays from its purpose the body of that kami becomes corrupted, as does its spirit. Ultimately that corruption results in the death of the body and the spirit. It is a process that begins with 罪 tsumi which leads to 穢れ kegare which ultimately leads to death 死 shi and the land of 黄泉 yomi.

Problems of society result from people violating the principles of 和 wa or harmony. Problems of the natural order stem from people upsetting the 神 kami. These offenses are a form of 罪 tsumi and result in 穢れ kegare.

The way to deal with 罪 tsumi and 穢れ kegare is the observance of proper ritual and offerings to repair the damaged relationship and to maintain the harmonious relationships that already exists within the community and with the 神 kami. The best life possible is achieved through these rituals for the community and the 神 kami.

However, Shintō realizes that 罪 tsumi and 穢れ kegare cannot be removed fully by those who are affected by 罪 tsumi and 穢れ kegare. The result of this inability is that the process of suffering and death is unending. The presence and effects of 穢れ kegare can be minimized, but not eliminated. There is a sense of hope for less suffering and greater purpose in life, but the elimination of suffering and fulfilling creative potential is impossible.

There are four main points of contact between the perceived, true need of Shintō and the Gospel: origin, impurity, purification, and spirits. Of these, the points of origin and impurity will be addressed in the next two chapters.

Chapter 4 Touchpoint: Creator

As demonstrated in the previous chapter, Shintō does not have a category for a creator. 結び *Musubi* has no personality, so trying to know 結び *musubi* is equivalent to trying to know the personality of the ocean. When one dies, their soul or spirit eventually returns to impersonal energy and joins impersonal 結び musubi. Without any hope for any resolution to this world's evil and suffering, it is possible to experience feelings of nihilism and despair. "It doesn't matter what I do or what has been done to me."

This is very similar to how the Stoics of Greece viewed the cycle of death and rebirth. Dr. David Cashin refers to them as cyclic pantheists. Doctor Cashin explained, "When Paul said that there was a creator and a judgment, an end to the cycle of death and rebirth, this was good news for the Stoics."

Before speaking of a judgment, Paul told the Greeks that there was a Creator. I believe that establishing a Creator is the first point of contact into a Seeker's heart, wherever they are from. 上帝 Jōtei is not a Creator who set the universe in motion and then left, but is present and gives purpose to human life.

To address this missing category, it is necessary to introduce the Japanese to the idea of a Creator God before introducing a name for Him. In the present translation of the Japanese Bible, the current word for YHWH is 神様 Kami-Sama, a term which many Japanese Christians admit is a difficulty. Differences between the Judeo-Christian and Shintō view of creation and Creator are represented in Figure 4.1.[1]

---

[1] Adapted from Paul G. Hiebert, "The flaw of the excluded middle." *Missiology* 10, no. 1 (January 1982): 35-47. *ATLA Religion Database with ATLASerials*, EBSCO*host* (accessed March 24, 2016), 40-44.

Shintō: the Gospel's Gate

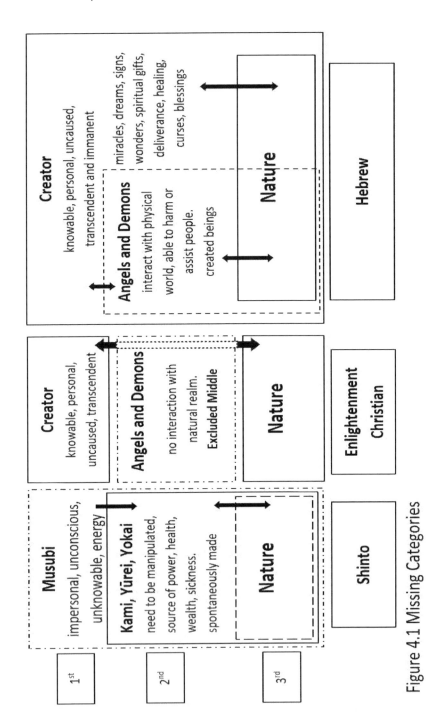

Figure 4.1 Missing Categories

Shintō: the Gospel's Gate

A possible solution is to look to China, from whom the Japanese borrowed the kanji writing system. Some of the present translations of the Bible into Chinese use the term 上帝 ShangDi, which, according to some sources, can be traced back to 2500 B.C.[2]

The curious thing is that the Japanese kept the characters for words that were used in the Japanese language, and "imported numerous words not in their spoken language, [though many of these] had similar meanings" (Boyle, written correspondence, Oct. 12, 2019). That the character for 上帝 ShangDi was kept with the Japanese pronunciation of Jōtei じょうてい suggests that at some point in history, the Japanese were aware of a creator, for whom Heavenly Emperor was appropriate. Chapter 13 discusses this issue further.

Jōtei

Using the name 上帝 Jōtei by itself does not solve the problem of the missing identity of a Creator. Instead of being stifled by the lack of a Creator God, it may be possible to use 結び musubi as a steppingstone to introduce the "unknown god".

There is something above the visible kami, but the Japanese have had little or no way to know who or what that something is. As a result, they take the agnostic approach and identify the source of creation as a mere energy source.

Acts 17 records two events where Paul was speaking to the Gentiles. In 17:7, the Thessalonians riot and bring charges that Paul was preaching against Caesar, that there was a new king named Jesus. Yet, in Acts 25 it is recorded that there are regional kings, namely Agrippa. So, if Paul were preaching another king, it would be more reasonable for the Thessalonians to say that Paul was spreading a message against the local king appointed by Caesar.

Although Paul's words to the Thessalonians were not recorded, when he reasoned with the Greeks in Athens, he used the Altar to the Unknown God as a steppingstone to introduce the Creator who had made himself personally known to the Hebrews. The words that Paul used were οὐρανοῦ

---

[2] Kong Hee, *God in Ancient China* (Singapore: Attributes Publishing, 2009, DVD).

καὶ γῆς κύριος[3] *ouranou kai ges kuriŏs* which is translated into English as "The Lord of Heaven and Earth."

For English readers, the term Lord is simply accepted as meaning one in authority, but a further check reveals κύριος *kuriŏs* means one who is supreme in authority: God, Lord, master.[4] For the time of the writing of Acts, the Emperor of Rome was the one in ultimate control of the government. Combining the reactions of the Thessalonians and the Athenians, the Greeks Paul was addressing seem to have understood Paul's description of the unknown god as "Emperor of Heaven and Earth."

The kanji of 上帝 Jōtei seem to be in harmony with the description of אֶלְיוֹן *el'elyon* "God Most High" or "God Above All" in Genesis 14:18, Isaiah 6:1-2, and Daniel 7:13-14.

In Daniel 7:13-14, YHWH is presented as being greater than kings whom we know in history as emperors. Also, in Daniel 4:25b-26 the Emperor of Babylon is told, "The Most High is ruler over the kingdoms of men, and He gives it to whom he wants . . . .. Your kingdom will be restored to you after you recognize that it is Heaven that rules."

The image derived from Daniel's confrontation with Nebuchadnezzar is that the Ruler of Heaven is also the Ruler of the kingdoms of the earth. Although מֶלֶךְ *melek* is usually translated as 'king', Hebrew does not have separate words for king and emperor, as demonstrated by scripture referring to the Emperor of Babylon as *Melek Babylon*. Speaking of YHWH as the Emperor of Heaven and Earth is in keeping with the imagery provided by the authors of Scripture.

Introducing Jōtei

There is the issue of how to introduce yet another name for the Creator God to the Japanese mind. 上帝 Jōtei is not unknown to the Japanese. In the past, I have simply started by writing the character for emperor 帝, asking

---

[3] F. H. A. Scrivener, *The New Testament in Greek* (Ac 17:24–25) (Cambridge: Cambridge University Press, 1881).

[4] James Strong, A Concise Dictionary of the Words in the Greek Testament and The Hebrew Bible (Vol. 1) (Bellingham: Logos Bible Software, 2009), 44.

the Japanese present what it means. Then I write the character above 上 and ask what the two characters mean together. This allows the Japanese to engage with the character in its pieces.

The Japanese database wwwjdic.com even offers the gloss of Supreme Being as a possible definition for 上帝 Jōtei.[5] Using the Japanese dictionaries to help introduce 上帝 Jōtei and it having been adopted by Buddhist monks in 700 A.D. establishes that this Emperor of Heaven is not a foreign god, even if He has been forgotten through the passage of time.

One possible objection is that 上帝 Jōtei sounds too distant and unapproachable, not the god of love described in Western Gospel presentations. However, to view YHWH simply through the distorted lens of the Western Gospel, who only wants everyone to have a good life, is to ignore vast quantities of the Old Testament where the very same Creator is presented as unapproachable (Exodus 19) and completely holy (set apart).

Jesus was not always a welcoming person – he turned over tables, whipped people, and called them thieves when he found them doing business within the Temple (John 2:15). While Jesus was quick to turn to those who cried for mercy, he was harsh with the Pharisees.

As a secondary concern, using 上帝 Jōtei does not require the Japanese Church to eliminate 神様 Kami-Sama. Our model can be taken directly from Scripture. When God first introduced himself to Abram, He did so with the name El Shaddai. Some centuries later, when He appeared to Moses, God revealed His personal name – Yahweh (see Exodus 6:3 with the Hebrew names).

When introducing the idea of a Creator God to the Japanese, we could start by introducing 上帝 Jōtei and then examining Genesis 1:1-13, Genesis 14:18-20, Isaiah 6:1-2, Daniel 7:13-14, and Daniel 4:25b-26, as mentioned above. One could then compare the account of YHWH and His Spirit hovering over the deep waters (Gen. 1:2) with the account in the opening of the Kojiki which introduces 天之御中主の神 Amenominakanushi no Kami.

---

[5] Jim Breen, http://www.edrdg.org/jmdictdb/cgi-bin/entr.py?svc=jmdict&sid=&q=1353950 accessed 6-10-16. Monash University.

Actually, 上帝 Jōtei is on-yomi. wwwjdic uses the hiragana characters, which led me to think that this was kun-yomi. Please see the chapter 11 in part 2 for details.

In this way, the Japanese understanding of YHWH as a Creator can be associated with the concept and title of 上帝 Jōtei, then be introduced to the Kojiki's account of 天之御中主 Amenominakanushi as the personal name of the Creator in Japanese cultural memory.

The term 神様 Kami-Sama could be used in the places of the Old Testament where Elohim appears in its singular sense as a title for YHWH. And then use 神 kami for those places where elohim appears in the plural sense.

Through such a method, the Japanese understanding of a Creator should be rather quick to form, the only remaining barrier being the ability to introduce 上帝 Jōtei into common usage. But this should present less difficulty than trying to explain a Creator as a 'leader of kami'.

Importance

One of the important reasons for being certain to introduce the knowledge of a Creator as the Emperor of Heaven and Earth is that, like all fear-based cultures, the Japanese are aware of the need to protect themselves from the presence of demons and angry 幽霊 yūrei, or ghosts. As demonstrated in figure 4.1, the Enlightenment Christian worldview excludes the presence of demons in the natural world. However, the Hebrew Scripture is full of the accounts about Satan and his demons' ability to affect the natural realm.[6]

Job 1-3 demonstrates an angelic being's ability to cause tornadoes, disease, and direct groups of people to attack. The Gospels likewise demonstrate demons' ability to cause mental disorders, disease, physical deformity, mutilations, and other torments. Without the authority to expel such spirits, people are forced to bargain with them or turn to other spirits who can overcome the effects of the spirit that is tormenting them.

This is the function and role of Shamans. While Shamans may seem like a distant reality from America, Americans rely on psychics, mediums, and Wiccans because the Enlightenment Church has abandoned their commission to expel evil spirits (Mark 16:15-17).

---

[6] see Michael S. Heiser, *Unseen Realm* (Bellingham: Lexham Press, 2015) for an extensive examination of the Hebrew view of the spirit world.

Shintō: the Gospel's Gate

For any people group, if there is no creator, no ultimate source of life, then life is simply about getting and maintaining power. As discussed in the previous chapter, in the case of Shintō, every living 神 kami eventually returns to 結び musubi and ceases to exist. In such case there is no hope for a life after death. As Paul succinctly quotes the Greeks, "If the dead are not raised, 'Let us eat and drink for tomorrow we die!'" (1 Corinthians 15:32, ESV). Yet, if there is a Creator who is the Ruler of Heaven and Earth, then there is the possibility of life after death.

Personalizing the Abstract

How to personalize an abstract idea like the Emperor of Heaven and Earth is a legitimate concern. There is something about an intellectual answer and debate that simply does not allow a person to personalize or respond emotionally to the reality of who 上帝 Jōtei is.

Scripture that contains images and poetic descriptions of 上帝 Jōtei will undoubtedly be the best source, for the seeker and the believer. There are a few recommendations that I will present here – they are not exhaustive and will not be appropriate for every situation, but they should provide an example. These exercises should be done by the person who is seeking to know who 上帝 Jōtei is.

1) Read Isaiah 6:1-2 and sketch the scene as Isaiah saw it. Meditate on the scene.

2) Read Daniel 4:25 and write five implications – personal or general – that can be made from this verse.

3) Read Job 36:22-37:16. Highlight or underline phrases that stand out to you. Take turns discussing one of these phrases with a co-student for at least five minutes per person.

4) Read Job chapter 38 verses 4-7, 8-11, 12-15, 16-18, 19-24, 25-30, 31-35, 36-41 in sections.

Read one section a day for eight days. During the day think about 上帝 Jōtei's ability to do these things. Is there any person who could do these things in their own power?

Day 1-8: Make small journal entries on your insights, emotional reactions, or observations each day.

Shintō: the Gospel's Gate

Day 9: Read Job 38:4-41 in its entirety. Do not take notes or journal.

Day 10: Review your journal entries. Take 30 minutes to write about your impressions, thoughts, emotions, or longings from this exercise.

Day 11: share your Day 10 writing with a co-student or mentor. Discuss and reflect to help each other process the experience.

There is, of course, more that could be said and researched about how to help people understand the concept of the Creator God. However, introducing the concept and category is enough for the present endeavor. Let us seek to avoid the trap of trying to prove or convince the seeker of the existence of a Creator. What good does it do us to win an argument but lose the soul? (1 Peter3:15)

To help the existence of a Creator relate to the individual's life, the next chapter explores relating Mosaic Law to the Shintō worldview.

CHAPTER 5 TOUCHPOINT: IMPURITY

In the last three chapters we examined the Shintō worldview and moved toward an understanding of why this author has chosen to use the name 上帝 Jōtei, Emperor of Heaven for the name of YHWH.

Having taken this step, we can revisit the principles of social and government harmony that are fundamental to Japanese sense of 和 wa. In list form the principles are:

   Do not be greedy
   Do not spread rumors
   Do not steal
   Do not have sex with someone else's spouse
   Do not murder
   Honor your family
   Celebrate the festivals for the kami and the Emperor
   Speak the Emperor's name with reverence
   Only serve the Emperor and his officials
   There is only one Emperor of Japan

These ten principles of 和 wa correlate to the Ten Commandments, Exodus 20:3-17, with slight re-wordings and in reverse order to the Scriptural form.

   Do not covet
   Do not bear false witness
   Do not steal
   Do not commit adultery
   Do not murder
   Honor your father and mother
   Remember the Sabbath and keep it holy, because the Emperor of Heaven set it apart

Shintō: the Gospel's Gate

> Do not use the Emperor of Heaven's name dishonorably
> Do not make for yourselves or serve any false emperors
> There is only one Emperor of Heaven

Asking the Japanese for the principles of 和 *wa*, and writing them down, should enable the discussion to examine how they parallel the Ten Commandments from Scripture. Then these are no longer foreign, unfamiliar commands, but express the 和 Wa of Heaven. As such, violating these principles brings disharmony and are acts of 罪 *tsumi* which result in 穢れ *kegare*.

We can examine the list of Heavenly and Earthly Tsumi to make the concerns of Shintō easier to discuss.[1] More will be said on this in ch 9.

Heavenly Tsumi	Earthly Tsumi
Destroying divisions between fields.	Skin irregularities in color, rashes, and warts.
Double planting of seeds.	Sex with animals.
Driving stakes into mud to cause injury.	Incest.
Spreading excrement over the doors.	Uncleanness by lightning.
Injuring the skin to cause blood to run.	Uncleanness by insects.
Desecrating a corpse.	Different sorts of incantation, witchcraft, curse, and divination.[1]

Table 5.1 Types of Tsumi

The First Transgression

It is relevant and necessary to establish where the first instance of mankind violating the Commands of Heaven occurred. For Shintō, the answer is in the events where Izanami gave birth to the Fire Kami, Kagutsuchi.

---

[1] Correlated from Katao Genchi, *A Study of Shintō* (Tōkyō: The Zaidan-Hōjin-Meiji-Seitoku-Kinen-Gakkai, 1926), 112-113, and *Japan Illustrated Encyclopedia vol. 1.* (New York: Kodansha America, 1993).

Shintō: the Gospel's Gate

When Izanagi traveled to the underworld, or Yomi, he returned and had to cleanse himself from the impurity of death, during which Amaterasu, Tsukuyomi, and Susano-o were brought into being.

The point of contact between Shintō and Hebrew creation stories for the origin of sin is the Serpent. As already discussed, the first man and woman were living in harmony with the Emperor of Heaven and it was the introduction of the Serpent that led to the first violation of this harmony.

Post Script: A Remembered Offense

It is an unpleasant task, but one that must be addressed. As the Church, Western Christians need to assess the contact between the nations and the Western Christian nations in light of the principles of community listed above.

As individuals we may have no direct link to the invasion force from Spain and Portugal around 1540, the Black Ships led by Commodore Perry, or the anti-Japanese attitudes that many missionaries brought with them in the 1950s; yet as a community of believers we share in that heritage. Individualistic Westerners generally lack a sense of group conscience, yet Japanese culture is acutely aware of this concept.

As Ezra led Israel in public confession of the sin of their forefathers, some seventy years previous, so the Western Church needs to examine our history. Of particular merit to my mind is Deuteronomy 19:14 against moving ancient boundary markers.

Conquering a nation and removing their wealth – *vis a vis* the United Kingdom – is certainly covered by this. The way of a culture is, in a sense, a boundary marker because it distinguishes one culture from another. In Acts 15, the Apostles and Elders wrote that the Gentiles did not have to change their culture, only to avoid food that had been strangled or sacrificed to idols, sexual immorality, and consuming blood.

How quick are we Gentiles to agree that the Hebrews should not place their culture on us! But are we such hypocrites that we intend to tell others that they must become Westerners in order to be Christians? Are we thieves that we try and steal a nations' natural resources and cultural identity to please ourselves? If we do these things to please ourselves, are we serving our appetites or 上帝 Jōtei?

What does an ethnically Japanese church look like? It is an exciting question, but the answer will only be discovered when the Japanese people are no longer held in bondage to Westernizers who add unnecessary burdens and offenses to the Gospel of Jesus Christ (1 Corinthians 10:31-33). If we are to reach out effectively to our neighbors and friends, we must value them as individuals and stop trying to make them look, talk, and act like we do in order to be 'proper' Christians.

Let us repent of the corporate sin and let us asses ourselves to see if this is a generational sin that we are carrying on in our own lives and ministry.

CHAPTER 6 PSALM 51

How did the Hebrew people understand the concept of sin? Earlier, I mentioned that the Greek understanding of sin is to 'miss the mark' and that definition seems to have been exported back into the Hebrew translation.

To understand this in as short a time period as possible, I decided to use an exegetical project on Psalm 51 for one of my Hebrew classes. The bulk of chapter 8 and 9 is working from that original paper, with some modifications for style and corrections with further study.

Please note that the discussion may get a little technical, however, it will allow readers to see the structure and beauty of David's writing.

David was the second king of Israel, and he is considered the greatest of the kings by later authors of 1 and 2 Kings and 1 and 2 Chronicles. But David was still human and 2 Samuel 11:1 – 12:17 tells a tragic story.

One day David remained at home instead of going to the battlefield. While on his roof, he saw the beautiful Bathsheba and had sex with her. She became pregnant, so David arranged to have her husband, Uriah, killed in battle. David married Bathsheba and concealed the affair and murder until after the baby was born.

Then one day, the prophet Nathan confronted David. During the confrontation YHWH spoke of David's actions as despising YHWH's commands and showing contempt for YHWH.

Psalm 51 is set some time after Nathan's confrontation and is categorized as a Lament Psalm, sub-grouped as a Psalm of Confession. In table 6.1 the psalm is arranged into three columns of five verses each. Column A contains verse 1-5, which is where the focus of our discussion will remain for part one.

	A	B	C
1	¹ Have mercy on me, Elohim. According to your faithful love and many mercies, cover my trespasses.	⁶ Behold your way delights the inward parts. You instruct me in wisdom.	¹¹ Do not cast me away from your presence. Do not take your Holy Spirit from me.
2	² Thoroughly wash me from my iniquity, purify me.	⁷ Cleanse my sin with hyssop, make me pure as snow.	¹² Return to me the joy of your salvation. Sustain me by your noble spirit.
3	³ Because my transgressions testify against me, my sin is always before me.	⁸ After you have crushed my bones, let me hear shouts of joy and gladness.	¹³ Then I will teach the transgressors your word. Those who have fallen away will return to you.
4	⁴ Against you alone I have sinned, entering evil before you. Therefore, you are righteous when you speak, pure in your judgment.	⁹ Remove my sin from before you, and all my iniquities wipe away.	¹⁴ Rescue me from [the curse of] bloodshed, Elohim, Mighty One of my Salvation, then my tongue will sing of your righteousness.
5	⁵ Behold, I have twisted authority and in sin the *mother* of *my* child conceived.	¹⁰ Create in me a new heart, renew *my trust* in Elohim.	¹⁵ Open my lips, Lord, then *my mouth* will proclaim your praise.

Table 6.1 Psalm 51

Structure and Translation

Psalm 51 has a pattern of movement established in 3 groups of 5 (columns A, B, and C) and 1 group of 2 verses.[1] This structure is called a strophe[2] which is defined as "being arranged by stanzas: a division of a poem consisting of a series of lines arranged together in a ... recurring pattern ...."[3] The underlined words in the translation above indicate the Hebrew words of this strophic pattern.

Each lateral line shares a common theme of progression: wash, cleanse, and return (row 2); testify, hear, and teach (row 3); enter, remove, rescue (row 4). Additionally, each strophe builds on the tension as it descends, and focuses on a particular stage of relationship. In Strophe A, David is confessing. In strophe B, David is asking El Shaddai to cleanse him. And in strophe C, David is describing his anticipated response to being restored.

My father	1 Samuel 24:11; 2 Kings 2:12, 5:13, 6:21, 13:14.
My daughter	Ruth 2:8 and 3:10
My son	Joshua 7:19; 1 Samuel 3:6, 24:16, 26:17, 26:21; 2 Samuel 18:22

Table 6.2 Honorifics

I have translated verse 5 as "the mother of my child" instead of "my mother" because: If it is translated as a confession of David being born in sin, the pattern is interrupted; If David is speaking in an honorific formula, referring to Bathsheba as 'my mother', the progression is maintained.

We find examples of an honorific formula for father, daughter, and son in table 6.2. These honorific forms take place in dialogue interceding or asking for favor with the person being addressed. The lack of honorific address to a

---

[1] Author's translation with help from reference materials, rendered for Hebrew 3 class at CIU.

[2] D. Witthoff, K. A. Lyle, & M. Nerdhal, ed. E. Evans, *Psalms Form and Structure* (Bellingham: Faithlife, 2014). Whittoff and others note that verses 18 and 19 were addendums to the poem.

[3] F. C. Mish, *Merriam-Webster's Collegiate Dictionary, Eleventh ed.* (Springfield: Merriam-Webster, Inc., 2003).

woman as 'my mother' could be explained by the majority of dialogue in Scripture being addressed to men or to YHWH. Also, a search of the Bible found no references for 'she gave birth to my son' or 'the mother of my son' in translation, so we have nothing to compare it to within the scriptural texts.

Additionally, David could be using this honorific address to maintain the First-person Active Singular נִ֫ "knee" ending on key terms and using the First-person Passive Singular תִ֫ "tee" ending in the horizontal progression of row 5 to maintain the subject agreement in the Hebrew language. While we are unaware of this dynamic in translation, it does have an effect in the original Hebrew sound and visual impression.

There is a second literary technique being employed.

The first line of each strophe speaks of some attribute or possession of El Shaddai; the last line of each strophe speaks of some attribute or possession of David. In such a way there is the continuation of the Hebrew pattern of poetic contrast helping to build tension and movement.

My final motivation for translating 'the mother of my child' instead of 'my mother gave birth to me' is because of the time focus of the poem. David is confessing his present state of sinfulness and the first strophe (column 1) is describing his act of rebellion against YHWH. For verse 5 to switch to David's state at birth completely alters the timeframe and such a change does not occur in the other two strophes. The skill and effort that David put into composing the stanzas and progression of the strophes laterally and vertically deserves to be considered in the process of translation.

One of the key verses for the Doctrine of Total Depravity is Psalm 51:5, translated as a confession of sinfulness from birth. To insist on a translation because of a doctrine is the very essence of eisegesis – interpreting scripture to fit a pre-determined meaning. For the scholar or pastor who holds a theology of Total Depravity, this author humbly asks for their longsuffering and patience.

Chapter 7 Psalm 51: Hebrew Words

In Psalm 51 David confesses that he has sinned and identifies that sin with the words פֶּשַׁע *pesha* violation or trespass, עָוֹן *awon* twist or iniquity, and חָטָא *hata* to miss or do wrong. These three words appear fifteen times in verses 1-10, while words relating to law are only mentioned once in all 17 verses. But the word for judgment שָׁפַט *shaphat* in verse 4 may not have legal connotations, since it can also mean 'assessment' or 'evaluation' in this usage.

Jenni and Westermann explain,

> עָוֹן *awon* occurs 248 times in the Old Testament in noun and verb form carrying the meaning to bend, curve, turn aside, twist . . . and is used to formally disqualify certain actions, behaviors, or circumstances and their consequences . . . so it is translated as guilt and iniquity.[1]

For Psalm 51 David is using עָוֹן *awon* to describe the misuse or twisting of his authority as King of Israel.[2] Such behavior could be expressed in English as a 'perversion of justice'.

פֶּשַׁע *pesha* occurs 134 times as a verb or noun in the Old Testament and has been primarily translated as transgression or crime.[3] Alternatively, it may refer to transgression or rebellion in the context of relationships.[4]

---

[1] E. Jenni and C. Westermann, *Theological Lexicon of the Old Testament* (Peabody: Hendrickson Publishers, 1997), 863.

[2] David's actions of summoning Bathsheba and having sex with her would be considered Authority Rape today. Parallel situations are teachers having sex with students, or a judge having sex in exchange for legal favors.

[3] E. Jenni, *Theological Lexicon of the Old Testament*, 1033.

Shintō: the Gospel's Gate

The noun transgression comes from the verb transgress, which can be broken down into the Latin roots of *trans* meaning to cross and *gress* meaning to go or walk, marking it as being similar in meaning to the word trespass: to be on property without permission.

Whereas the boundary in trespass is physical, the boundary in transgress may be relational, so violating a cultural standard, breaking a covenant, or withholding something expected as part of the relationship are all possible implications of the word transgression. For Psalm 51 this transgression is in David violating the marriage covenant between Uriah and Bathsheba and violating the covenant with YHWH by adultery and murdering Uriah by proxy (2 Sam. 11:14-15).

חָטָא *chata* occurs 595 times in the Old Testament and is translated as 'sin'. In Psalm 51 it first appears after David confesses פֶּשַׁע *pesha* in verse 1 and עָוֹן *awon* in verse 2, giving an impression that sin is defined by the act of transgression and twisting.

The standard definition of חָטָא *chata* is given as 'to miss the mark' stemming from the translation of Judges 20:16 "they [the slingers] all hurled stones and hit precisely, without missing."[5] But the word 'missing' could easily be replaced with the word 'error' or 'being deceived' to express the slingers' accuracy.

For instance, the sport of golf sometimes speaks of a deceptive layout of a course, or in driving one may speak of a deceptive corner. This is merely to point out that defining חָטָא *chata* as missing the mark based on one verse in the Old Testament (where that translation is not required) presents reasonable opportunity to question the accuracy of the definition.

Between the alternatives of deception and error, error seems to best fit Judges 20:16. Here, the complexity and history of the English language come into play. In modern usage error means 'to make a mistake' but the term error is derived from 'err':

err \'er, 'ər\ verb intransitive
[Middle English, from Anglo-French errer, from Latin errare to wander, err;

---

[4] F. D. Bianchi, et al (editors), *Lexham Theological Wordbook:* Rebelliousness. (Bellingham: Lexham Press, 2014).

[5] E. Jenni, *Theological lexicon of the Old Testament*, 407.

akin to Old English ierre wandering, perverse, Gothic airzeis deceived] 14th century
1 archaic: STRAY
2a: to make a mistake
2b: to violate an accepted standard of conduct.[6]

The above definition uses the term perverse, which correlates to עָוֹן *awon* and 2b is the definition of transgression which correlates to פֶּשַׁע *pesha*. Adding credibility, it is noted that the inner-causative (*hiphil*) of חָטָא *chata* is "to let oneself err, fail . . . the criterion for "error" is not particular commandments but injury to a communal relationship."[7]

In this sense, David's petition in verse 11, "Do not take the Holy Spirit from me", is expressing a breach of relationship with YHWH. In this way err as 'violating a relationship' is an appropriate interpretation of חָטָא *chata*.

Another consideration is the pictographic nature of Hebrew in its original, pre-Babylonian form, often referred to as Paleo Hebrew. Hebrew letters have names which relate to an object – for example י *yod* was the picture of an arm representing strength. According to this theory, the meaning of the base word can be demonstrated by examining the meaning of the pictures of the letters. Thus, each word is a pictograph, much like the radicals of Chinese characters combine to form new kanji with particular meanings. In the case of חָטָא *chata* the pictograph suggests 'life separated from God by the serpent'.

The Greek understanding of ἁμαρτάνω *hamartano* 'sin' as 'to miss a mark' still needs to be addressed. Strong's Concordance defines *hamartano* (G264) with: 1) to be without a share; 2) to miss the mark; 3) to err, be mistaken; 4) to wander from the path of uprightness and honor; 5) to wander from the law, to violate God's law, sin.[8]

The first part of the definition, 'to be without a share' expresses the idea 'to be separated or excluded from a relationship or a reward'. Even more

---

[6] F. C. Mish, *Merriam-Webster's Collegiate Dictionary*.

[7] E. Jenni, *Theological lexicon of the Old Testament*, 406, 409.

[8] https://www.blueletterbible.org/lang/lexicon/lexicon.cfm? Strongs=G264&t=KJV accessed 3/19/16.

important are the expression of part 3 and 4 which align with the definitions of חָטָא *chata* and פֶּשַׁע *pesha*. Further, if we think of God's law as a prescription for the proper way to live life relationally, physically, and morally, then wandering from God's law could be summarized as perverting life – עָוֹן *awon*.

Such a consideration demonstrates that there is no conflict between the Old Testament and the New Testament view of sin. The problem lies with the Western legal point of view.

Other References

The reliability and consistency of the terms עָוֹן *awon*, פֶּשַׁע *pesha*, and חָטָא *chata* need to be investigated to determine if there is a pattern in Scripture that support the use of these terms for defining sin. A search using the terms in Logos returned four verses using both פֶּשַׁע *pesha* and חָטָא *chata*, thirteen verses using both עָוֹן *awon* and חָטָא *chata*, and eighteen verses for פֶּשַׁע *pesha* and עָוֹן *awon*. This is only looking for these three words and does not include parallel terms such as abandon עָזַב *azav*; therefore, it is not a comprehensive list. Also, bear in mind that the verse numbers and chapters were not original to the writing of Scripture. Some of the verses contained all three of the terms and so are counted multiple times in the numbers above.

Verses that contain at least two of the three terms are included in the list below, indicating that Scripture has a definite link between the concepts of stray, twist, and err. Verses are from LEB.

Leviticus 16:21 And Aaron shall place his two hands on the living goat's head, and he shall confess over it all the Israelites' iniquities עָוֹן and all their transgressions פֶּשַׁע for all their sins חָטָא.

Isaiah 1:4 Ah, sinful חָטָא nation, a people heavy with iniquity עָוֹן, offspring of evildoers, children who deal corruptly. They have forsaken Yahweh; they have despised the holy one of Israel. They are estranged and have gone backward.

Isaiah 53:5 But he was pierced because of our transgressions פֶּשַׁע, crushed because of our iniquities עָוֹן.

Isaiah 59:12 For our transgressions פֶּשַׁע are numerous before you, and our sins חָטָא testify against us. Indeed, our transgressions פֶּשַׁע are with us, and we know our iniquities עָוֺון.

Psalm 32:5 I made known my sin חָטָא to you, and my iniquity עָוֺון I did not cover. I said, "I will confess concerning my transgressions פֶּשַׁע to Yahweh," and you took away the guilt עָוֺון of my sin חָטָא.

Job 13:23 "How many are my iniquities עָוֺון and sins חָטָא? Make known to me my transgression פֶּשַׁע and my sin חָטָא.

Ezekiel 21:24 Because you have brought to remembrance your guilt עָוֺ by the uncovering of your transgressions פֶּשַׁע, so that your sins חָטָא in all of your deeds appear . . ..

Jeremiah 33:8 And I will cleanse them from all their guilt עָוֺון that they sinned חָטָא against me, and I will forgive all their iniquities עָוֺ that they sinned חָטָא against me, and that they rebelled פֶּשַׁע against me.

Daniel 9:24 to put an end to the transgression פֶּשַׁע and to seal up sin חָטָא and to make atonement for guilt עָוֺון.

Hebrew Understanding of Sin

According to the Hebrew mind the definition of sin is any action which twists the good things of 上帝 Jōtei's creation, or by which we transgress the boundaries established by relational covenant. For Israel, the Ten Commandments set the boundaries of transgression and can be labeled as moral or ethical sin because they violate the laws of the community.

A second form of sin in the Hebrew mind is addressed extensively in the books of Leviticus and Numbers. These forms of transgression and twisting deal with things that make a person physically unclean: issue of blood or semen, childbirth, dead bodies, infectious diseases, graves, certain animals, sex with animals, incest, any form of sorcery, and presenting unauthorized offerings.

Table 7.1 compares the Shintō expression of 罪 *tsumi* with the Hebrew understanding of violations that closely parallel them. The theme is community harmony and personal purity.

In the table, Scripture lists necromancy as a distinct branch of magic. Most commentaries and definitions relate it as being a form of mediumship or clairvoyance to speak with the dead. I propose that this understanding is redundant since divination and mediumship have already been listed.

Instead, the definition I suggest is that necromancy is a branch of magic that is concerned with drawing power or casting spells using items associated with death. Casting spells in a graveyard to harness the spirits of death, using earth taken from a grave in rituals, attempting to collect or manipulate the souls of the dead through any means (hair, fingernails, blood, tissue, or items collected from dead bodies) in charms, rituals, and incantations, sex with the dead (necrophilia) and even eating parts of the dead would be included in necromancy.[9]

Result of Sin

In Scripture a violation of one of these standards and committing sin חָטָא *chata* does not necessarily result in a change in legal status. Instead, it results in טֻמְאָה *tumah* uncleanness or impurity, which occurs some 160 times in the Old Testament, along with three other related terms.[10] This impurity in Hebrew thought can be directly related to the Shintō concept of 穢れ *kegare*.

Phonetically, טֻמְאָה *tumah* sounds like the English word tumor, pronounced without the 'r' sound. Taking small liberties, then, Westerners could relate the concept of טֻמְאָה and 穢れ *kegare* as a form of spiritual cancer, which makes us unclean.

While the Shintō worldview understands that this spiritual cancer separates us from our creative potential, Hebrew thought understands טֻמְאָה

---

[9] See John Ramirez, *Out of the Devil's Cauldron* and Mark Andrew Richie, *Spirit of the Rainforest*.

[10] E. Jenni, *Theological lexicon of the Old Testament*, 496.

tumah as something that separates us from our Creator.

There are a myriad of verses which speak about impurity in various ways: spot, blemish, dross, impurity, stain, scarlet, and corruption to name a few. When Isaiah is confronted with a vision of 上帝 Jōtei, he cries out because of his unclean lips (Isaiah 6:5). While Westerners may associate impurity with the color black, Isaiah 1:18 associates impurity with red, comparing the stains to scarlet and crimson.

Shintō	Hebrew
Destroying divisions between fields.	Deut. 19:14 Do not remove an ancient boundary marker which your ancestors made.
Double planting of seeds.	Lev 19:19 You will not sow two different kinds of seed.
Driving stakes into mud to cause injury.	Exodus 21:33-34 If a man opens a pit . . . and he does not cover it and an ox or a donkey falls into it, the owner of the pit will pay restitution.
Spreading excrement over the doors.	Deut. 23:13 Use a digging tool and dig a hole when you relieve yourself and then cover your [waste].
Injuring the skin to cause blood to run.	Deut. 14:1 You must not injure yourself for the dead.
Desecrating a corpse.	Numbers 19:16 Anyone . . . who touches . . . a corpse, or a bone of a person, or a burial site, he will be unclean for seven days.
Skin irregularities in color, rashes, and warts.	Leviticus 13:1-46
Sex with animals.	Lev. 18:23 You shall not have sex with any animal
Incest.	Lev. 18:1-18
Uncleanness by lightning.	None.
Uncleanness by insects.	Deut. 14:19 And also all of the winged insects; they are unclean for you; you shall not eat them.
Different sorts of incantation, witchcraft, curse, and divination, are abundantly mentioned in old Shintō documents.	Deut. 18:10-11 You shall not practice divination, or make magic charms, or cast spells, or consult the dead, or practice necromancy.

Table 7.1 Ritual Impurity

CHAPTER 8 DIAGNOSING SIN

One of the difficulties of explaining the concept of sin in Japanese culture is its normal understanding as crime. While we cannot undo the use of this kanji, we can use narrative reframing to tell a story with 罪 *tsumi* to help explain the concept. In this chapter we will introduce a diagnostic questionnaire and two graphs which can express the two concepts of 罪 *tsumi* and 穢れ *kegare* visually, to help make it easier to share and to personalize.

After using the Story of Tsumi[1] and the Shame Triad for almost two years, I have found that it is better to use the diagnostic tool first, then the Story of Tsumi, and finally using the Shame Triad to explain the effects of 罪 *tsumi* on the individual. This provides a smoother transition from personal to biblical, then back to personal.

In a way, this lays the foundation for a diagnosis before the seeker knows that there is a disease being diagnosed. I think psychologists would refer to this as a blind test. Our intention is not to trick or to shame our friend. We are bypassing the normal defensiveness when discussing sin. A diagnosis helps them to see and understand the reality instead of trying to argue the seeker into agreement.

Diagnostic Questionnaire

A little humor and a common scenario can be used to reveal the presence of 罪 *tsumi* and 穢れ *kegare* in the Seeker. A sample dialogue is provided below, with the Evangelist writing key terms on one side of a piece of paper

---

[1] The Story of Tsumi was originally published in a newsletter for Second Level Ministry on March 21, 2016, written by Brian T. McGregor.

as it progresses.

> E: Did your mother ever buy cookies and tell you that you couldn't have any until after dinner?
> S: Yes.
> E: Did you ever eat one anyway?
> S: (Laughter) Yes, of course.
> E: What motivated you to take the cookie?
> S: I was greedy.
> E writes "greed".
> E: After you ate the cookie were you proud of yourself?
> S: No, I felt shame.
> E writes "shame"
> E: Were you afraid of what would happen when your mom found out you ate the cookie?
> S: Yes.
> E writes "fear"
> E: When your mom found out, did you have conflict?
> S: Yes.
> E writes "strife"

It is important that we allow the Seeker to use their own words; however, the Shame Triad uses specific terminology. Therefore, if the Seeker uses a related term, such as "I was scared" the Evangelist could suggest the term Fear. With the Seeker's agreement, the keyword can be written down without pressuring the Seeker for the keyword.

At the end of this question and answer, there is simply the four words on one side of the paper. The kanji for 罪 *tsumi* can then be drawn in the empty space and the Shame Triad below 罪 *tsumi*.

Reframing Tsumi

As stated before, one obstacle to discussing sin with the Japanese is that the word 罪人 *tsumibito* means criminal and is the word used for sinner. For the majority of Japanese, being told that they are a sinner is the same as being told that they are a criminal. One way to deal with this is to give a new meaning to 罪 *tsumi*. I suggest doing this by using it to tell the story of Genesis 3.[2]

Shintō: the Gospel's Gate

As stated in the beginning of this book, the record of Genesis sets the tone and crisis for Scripture. When the first couple were tempted by Satan, they saw that the Knowledge of Good and Evil was desirable and took the fruit that had been placed off-limits.

They transgressed 上帝 Jōtei's boundary. When they ate the fruit and took the knowledge they wanted, they were misusing a good thing that 上帝 Jōtei had created. They were separated from 上帝 Jōtei's presence and became unclean. Considering these things, we can use the character of 罪 tsumi to tell the story of the origin of impurity.

The Story of Tsumi

The Story of Tsumi offers a chronological examination of the first sin recorded in Scripture. This rebellion resulted in separation from the Creator, who is the source of purity, creativity, and life.

Like most kanji, 罪 tsumi is made of separate radicals put together to form another concept. Checking in Rikaichan and WWWJDIC, the upper character in 罪 tsumi represents a net, 网 amigashira, radical number 122 and is used in 109 kanji. However, it only appears in the box form which resembles an eye 目 me on its side. The second radical is listed as number 175, 非 hi, and originally carries the meaning of contradiction or injustice.

For the purposes of this narrative reframing, once the radical root of 罒 as 网 has been established, the narrative can be told. The kanji 罪 is being used as a map, a skeleton upon which to tell the story.

There is no sense in which we are trying to change the meaning of 罪 tsumi, only that we are using it as a tool to help explain the origin of the problem of this world. As the narrative is told, the evangelist should write the parts of the kanji on a piece of paper. The stroke order is indicated to the right of each line in Table 8.1.

---

[2] Inspired by C. H. Kang and Ethel R. Nelson, *The Discovery of Genesis: How the Truths of Genesis Were Found Hidden in the Chinese Language* (St. Louis: Concordia Publishing House, 1979), 64.

Shintō: the Gospel's Gate

At this point, even if the Seeker does not become a follower of Jesus, we have succeeded in explaining sin as a matter of violating relationship, rather than breaking laws. Hopefully, whenever they see 罪 *tsumi* written down, they will remember this story from Scripture.

The Story of Tsumi	Strokes
In the beginning, 上帝 Jyōtei created man and he put the man in a garden. 上帝 Jyōtei's way was straight and true. |	|
He told the man three things: 1) You may eat from any tree — 2) Except from the Tree of Knowledge — 3) Or you will die —	𦣻
One day, 上帝 Jyōtei's enemy, the serpent, came into the garden and approached the man. The serpent laid a trap. 网	⌈XX⌉ 𦣻
The serpent twisted God's words. 丿 He said: 1) You do not have the best — 2) You will not die — 3) You will be gods —	⌈XX⌉ 非
The man listened to the enemy and ate the forbidden fruit. He was separated from God, and died. This separation has been handed down from the first man to his children, to their children, to us.	

Table 8.1 Story of Tsumi

Shame Triad

A second consideration is what happened in the hearts of the first man and woman.

When the Serpent told them the benefits of eating the fruit, they became greedy. As soon as they ate, the first couple were aware of their nakedness, expressing shame. Because of their shame, they felt fear when they heard 上帝 Jōtei walking in the garden and hid. When they were confronted about why they were hiding, the man began to blame 上帝 Jōtei and the woman, who in turn blamed the Serpent. This can be expressed in one word – strife.

Figure 8.1 shows the effect of 罪 *tsumi* in the spirit of the man and woman. They were now impure before 上帝 Jōtei. The first man and woman were separated from their creator, their labor was cursed, and they began suffering the corruption of death.

Figure 8.1 Shame Triad

Shintō: the Gospel's Gate

穢れ *kegare* encompassed all aspects of their lives: their relationship with the Creator, creation, family, and their created purpose. They would no longer have the ease and pleasure of work, or the harmony of the relationship they had enjoyed. When these elements are included in the graph, its final form is shown in figure 8.2. It is the image of the spiritual impurity that separates us from the Creator and our created purpose.

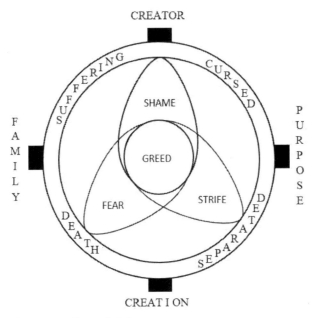

Figure 8.2 Effects of Kegare

One way to think of this impurity is that it is a type of spiritual cancer, a hereditary disease, handed down from father to child. While a child may be born without this spiritual cancer, if they live long enough, it will manifest in their lives. Even without having the disease active in their spirit, everyone is affected by the presence of impurity in the world.

Personalizing the Triad

With our seeker friend, we should pause and draw lines from their admission of greed, shame, fear, and strife to the appropriate petals of the Shame Triad shown in figure 8.1. No one wants to admit having an illness unless they see the symptoms in their own body.

With a disease like טֻמְאָה *tumah* and 穢れ *kegare* the symptoms are spiritual. With the diagnostic questionnaire, the seeker has already admitted to the symptoms of 穢れ *kegare* in their own heart. By changing how we talk about sin from a criminal act to a disease, it is no longer about a moral failure on the part of the person who is sick.

Even so, confronting a patient with a terminal diagnosis is not an easy task. The doctor does not simply enter the patient's room and tell them bluntly that they are dying from cancer. A test is conducted, and the doctor reviews the results with the patient. Then, as gently as possible the doctor informs the patient of the diagnosis of the disease and the prognosis.

Through such a method it is not the Christian trying to convince their friend that they have a disease. The symptoms are noted and the seeker is able to make their own diagnosis. It becomes their reality. It is at this point that the doctor leaves the patient alone so that they can process the emotions and reality of having a terminal disease.

Only after patients have accepted this new reality are they in a place to start learning about the treatment options. Our seeker friend may want to hear the diagnosis several times. The grieving process may manifest itself after hearing such news. The Christian must remain patient and allow their friend to come to them when they are ready to move forward in dealing with the spiritual cancer.

Shintō: the Gospel's Gate

CHAPTER 9 CONCLUSION PART 1

We have been examining how to correlate the concept of sin to the Japanese mind. To do this we have had to revisit how we think about the story of Scripture, focusing on the Genesis account as our foundation. In examining the Shintō worldview, we discovered that there is not a category for a Creator. As a result, when Christians use the term 神様 Kami-Sama without establishing a Creator, it creates a contradiction of terms for most Japanese people.

By being sensitive and respectful of Shintō perspectives, we found a simple way to introduce the Creator category and found a native title for him, 上帝 Jōtei. Thanks to work by Dr. Kikawa and others, we know that the native name for 上帝 Jōtei is 天之御中主 Amenominakanushi, The Divine Lord of the Very Center of Heaven.

During the act of creation, spiritual beings were created and one of them rebelled and became Satan, the Serpent who tempted the first man and woman into rebelling against 上帝 Jōtei, which caused human death and impurity to enter the world.

Actions which violate harmony 和 wa are acts of 罪 tsumi which result in 穢れ kegare, impurity. We have further demonstrated that 罪 tsumi is related to the Hebrew terms עָוֺן ayon, פֶּשַׁע peshah, and חָטָא chata, which result in טֻמְאָה tumah. Using the phonetic similarity, we have related טֻמְאָה tumah to spiritual cancer. Then we developed the Story of Tsumi and diagnostic test, the Shame Triad, to gently confront our seeker friends with the reality of their impurity.

We can summarize the process like this:
1. Violating the principles of 和 wa cause relational separation (חָטָא chata and 罪 tsumi)

2. חָטָא *chata* and 罪 *tsumi*, and violations of Shintō and Levitical purity laws, result in a state of impurity, called טֻמְאָה *tumah* and 穢れ *kegare*
3. טֻמְאָה *tumah* and 穢れ *kegare* are passed down from father to child and separate us from our creative potential and our Creator.

At this point of the story, the Serpent has taken away the special relationship 上帝 Jōtei had with the man and woman. The Creator's honor has been subjectively diminished. The man and woman now live in a state of shame and the impurity of death.

The conflict in the Garden concludes with 上帝 Jōtei expelling the man and woman from the Garden and putting enmity between the promised seed of the woman and the Serpent. In this conflict one will emerge victorious. Will 上帝 Jōtei bring resolution and restore His honor? What can be done to remove 穢れ *kegare* from the man and woman?

An American evangelist will be inclined to press directly to the cure, but this would be a critical mistake. Our seeker friend must be allowed to take time to process this new understanding of sin. For the seeker, there is the new reality of a Creator, a personal evil, the story of creation and the fall through the Story of Tsumi, and the diagnosis of sin within their own lives through the Shame Triad.

The seeker may respond in one of three ways: first, to remove themselves from the relationship; second, to ask about the cure; and third, they may pursue a better understanding of Shintō. Either way, the evangelist has succeeded in presenting the theistic worldview and a Hebraic-Christian understanding of sin.

PART 2: FROM DEATH TO LIFE

"I assure you: Anyone who hears my word and believes him who sent me has eternal life and will not come under judgment but has passed from death to life."
    ---- John 5:24 (HCSB)

Shintō: the Gospel's Gate

CHAPTER 10: CRISIS AND RESOLUTION

In part one we introduced the concept of an honor challenge, the Story of Tsumi, and the Shame Triad. Part one concluded with the exhortation to leave seekers in a state of crisis while they process this new understanding of sin and its presence in their lives. Part two will examine the solution to the problem.

In drama there are four possible resolutions to an honor challenge. The first option is that the loss of honor continues without being restored. This is what Adam and Eve experienced after being expelled from the Garden of Eden. The second option is that the claimant restores their honor to its original state. This is what happens when David retakes his kingdom from Absalom. The third option is that the claimant answers the challenge and their honor is enhanced. This is what happens with Joseph.

The fourth option is the most complicated and is often used as a structure for movies and books. The claimant answers the challenge, their honor is enhanced, the challenger renews the challenge and the claimant suffers greater loss, but then overcomes the new challenge and the claimant's honor is permanently enhanced, as diagramed in figure 10.1.

This more complicated honor challenge is the graph for Job's trial under Satan's torment. It is also the graph for how 上帝 Jōtei answer's Satan's challenge. I want to examine the motivation of Satan and Adam for their rebellion against 上帝 Jōtei.

Satan's challenge to Adam against 上帝 Jōtei was grounded in four aspects. Adam could be his own god and have honor, power, and control over the world separate from 上帝 Jōtei.

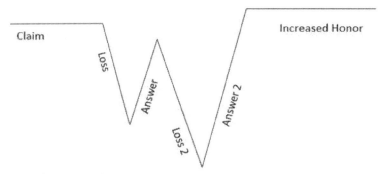

Figure 10.1 Increased Honor

This is exactly what Satan himself was trying to obtain when he rebelled against 上帝 Jōtei sometime between the creation of man and the temptation in the garden. Visually it can be represented in figure 10.2.

One critical flaw in this self-centered triad is that earned honor, power, and control can be lost. When someone steals or kills, they do so because they are putting their self above all others.

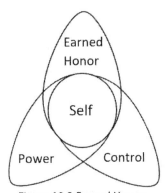

Figure 10.2 Earned Honor

We need to earn honor to cover our shame, have power to minimize our fear, and have control to take away others' ability to control us. Yet the fear of death is one fear that can never be overcome with earned honor, power, and control. It is this fear of death that truly pushes people to continue this cycle of rebellion.

This may sound strange, but we must look at it properly. Shame, fear, and strife are the result of greed, and express the fallen state of humanity. But the motivation for greed, the desired outcome of selfish behavior, is to gain those things which we do not have. To enhance our sense of self. People are not motivated to obtain those things that they already have.

For instance, consider all the things in our lives that we have worked hard to obtain. When we did not have that thing – a car, fame, or money – we believed we would be happy if we could just get that thing. Yet, once we obtained it, the satisfaction and honor soon tarnished because we encountered something – or someone – else which made what we had look inferior.

"If I can accomplish this, I'll be happy" is the mantra of many successful people. But soon enough the feeling of emptiness, the feeling of shame returns.

There was only one place where this feeling of shame was unknown. In the Garden of Eden, because 上帝 Jōtei was the source of Adam and Eve's honor. They had no need to earn honor since it was freely given. Their honor had been stative, coming from who they were and not what they were doing or what they had.

In many ways, the story of Creation must end where it began – in the Garden. But the second garden will be better than the first in that the challenge by Satan has been answered. The honor of humanity who were loyal to 上帝 Jōtei will be enhanced, and the subjective honor of 上帝 Jōtei will also be enhanced because He overcame Satan's challenge.

Adam and Eve were driven from the Garden with the anticipation that 上帝 Jōtei would defeat Satan. In the next several chapters, we will examine how 上帝 Jōtei revealed His answer through Israel and the Japanese.

Shintō: the Gospel's Gate

CHAPTER 11: JŌTEI REVISITED

Regarding 上帝 Jōtei, it was confirmed that this is an on-yomi character. However, this may be in the favor of using 上帝 Jōtei as the name for the Creator God in Japan. One repeated concern that has been expressed by Japanese Christians is that it may cause confusion based on the historical view that the Emperor of Japan was divine.

Because 上帝 Jōtei is on-yomi it cannot refer to the Japanese Emperor; and in fact, the Japanese do not use 帝 in reference to the Japanese Emperor. As a result, it immediately requires that the Japanese be introduced to the historical understanding of 上帝 ShangDi in China as the Creator God.

This is a good thing in that there is more than four thousand years of history and much written documentation about the identity of 上帝 ShangDi who is understood to be the same as El Shaddai from the Hebrew Scriptures.

While it is not a native Japanese term, China is a respected cultural neighbor to Japan and demonstrates that the Creator God is not a Western concept. A further positive consideration is to ask why the Japanese chose to keep 上帝 Jōtei in the kanji which were borrowed from China.

One reason I thought 上帝 Jōtei was kun-yomi is because the phonetics do not follow the normal pattern of borrowing the Chinese pronunciation for on-yomi. In the pattern of adoption that I can see, 上帝 ShangDi into Japanese phonetics should normally be Shaddai, not Jōtei.

As demonstrated through historical documents, the Keikyo Christians were active in China at the time the Japanese Buddhists were there developing the kanji system.[1] Since the kanji were being adapted to the Japanese language, the Buddhists were able to choose how the words should

---

[1] Samuel Lee, *Rediscovering Japan, Reintroducing Christendom: Two Thousand Years of Christian History in Japan* (New York: Hamilton Books, 2010), Kindle location 1589 of 3457.

be pronounced. It is my theory that the motivation for using Jōtei instead of Shaddai is because they recognized the similarity in sound to that of El Shaddai, which the Keikyo Christians would have immediately recognized as the name for God first revealed to Abraham.

However, Dr. Timothy Boyle introduced a second explanation, which I think has more merit.[2] Standard Chinese changed as the dynasties rose and fell. It is therefore reasonable to conclude that 上帝 Jōtei is an honest adaptation of the pronunciation that the Chinese were using at the time. In such case, 上帝 Jōtei is identical to 上帝 ShangDi, it simply traces to a different dialect of Chinese which was spoken during the Tang Dynasty.

A possible dialect came to my attention in June of 2019. I met with a man, whom I will call "Lao" for his safety, who had grown up on the Island of Xia'men (known in Japan as Amoi Island), where they speak Amoi Yu, also known as Mingnan Yu. When I told "Lao" about Jōtei, he responded, "This is very similar to the Amoi pronunciation of ShongDei. That's very similar, don't you think?"

Interestingly, some online Japanese dictionaries provide an alternate pronunciation of 上帝 Jōtei as Shōtei, providing a much stronger phonetic link. For those who want to follow further, Jay told me that Taiwan has a dictionary of Amoi written in Pinyin as developed by missionaries in Xia'men.

As such, I believe that rendering 上帝 ShangDi into Japanese as Shaddai can be employed by Japanese Christians today. It is simply explained as mirroring the current Chinese pronunciation of the Creator God and linking it to the Hebrew pronunciation which Yahweh (YHWH from now on) uses when He first introduces Himself to Abraham. Otherwise Jōtei or Shōtei are also viable.

To guard against confusion as to the identity of 上帝 Jōtei, the strategy of examining the Scriptures for references to Shaddai as the Emperor of Heaven and Earth need to be followed. One of the most striking is found in Daniel 4:37. As Nebuchadnezzar finishes his account of his insanity and restoration, he says, "I, Nebuchadnezzar, praise and exalt and honor the king of heaven, for all his works are truth, and his ways are justice." (LEB)

The Hebrew word מֶלֶךְ *melek* can be translated as emperor or king, so the

---

[2] Timothy Boyle, Facebook post 08-24-18

translation of the above verse could legitimately read, "I, Nebuchadnezzar, praise and exalt and honor the Emperor of Heaven." While the concern about confusion of 上帝 Jōtei referring to a Japanese Emperor is legitimate, introducing the Scriptural usage and the Chinese history of the term should sufficiently guard against this confusion taking a foothold.

Another consideration is the history of biblical interpretation in Japan and China. Today, 上帝 ShangDi is widely used in China as the name for the Creator God. This may be one of the many reasons that Christianity has been able to spread so widely within China as the Church became largely indigenous with the foreign missionaries being expelled by the government.

I would expect that if a Chinese Christian were to translate the Scriptures into Japanese, they would by default use 上帝.

Doron B. Cohen describes how the British originally used 上帝 ShangDi in their first translations of the Bible into Chinese, but eventually yielded to the American use of 神 shen. If the British system had been followed in Japan during the 1800s 上帝 Jōtei would have been the name used originally. Cohen further comments that the American missionaries ignored the true meaning of 神 kami in Japanese language and culture.[3]

Historical evidence is provided by Sidney Gulick, who was a missionary in Japan from 1887 to 1913. He served as a professor and lecturer in Doshisha University in Kyoto (1906-1913) and at the Imperial University in Kyoto (1907-1913). In 1934 he was decorated by the Emperor of Japan with the Third Class order of Meiji Decoration of Sacred Treasure.[4] In his book *Evolution Of The Japanese, Social And Psychic*, published in 1903, Gulick writes, "Consider the Chinese expression 'Jo-Tei,' which the Christians of Japan freely use for God; it means literally 'Supreme Emperor,' and refers to the supreme ruler of the universe."[5]

---

[3] Doron B. Cohen, *The Japanese Translations of the Hebrew Bible: History, Inventory, and Analysis* (Boston: Brill Academic Publishers, Inc, 2013), 26.

[4] Greg Robinson, "Sidney Gulick,"Densho Encyclopedia https://encyclopedia.densho.org/Sidney%20Gulick/ (accessed April 13, 2019).

[5] Sidney Lewis Gulick, *Evolution Of The Japanese, Social And Psychic* (New York: Fleming H. Revell Company, 1903) Kindle Locations 5813-5815.

A hidden benefit to using 上帝 Jōtei is that the Japanese have no emotional connection to the word. That is, there is no history of interpretation that must be overcome to reframe its meaning. Since 上帝 Jōtei is largely unknown and the Japanese do not have a previous understanding of it, the Hebrew understanding of El Shaddai could be readily attached to 上帝 Jōtei.

At least one dictionary gives the definition for 上帝 Jōtei as God; the Lord; Providence; the Creator; Supreme Being; the Absolute; the King of Kings.[6] There are also electronic dictionaries available which define 上帝 Jōtei as Yahweh. With such references, it seems that using 上帝 Jōtei would not be developing entirely new ground, but simply catching up to a cultural understanding which has been overlooked or dismissed by some interpreters.

Acts 17:26-27 reads, "And he made from one man every nation of humanity to live on all the face of the earth, determining their fixed times and the fixed boundaries of their habitation, [27] to search for God, if perhaps indeed they might feel around for him and find him. And indeed, he is not far away from each one of us" (LEB). If this scripture is correct, then 上帝 Jōtei appointed Japan's dominion and He is present within Japanese culture.

Yet another benefit addresses the Confucian idea that everyone must be in their correct place. As a foreign deity, 神様 Kami-Sama has no place in Japanese culture. Yet 上帝 Jōtei as the Emperor of Heaven reigns above the Emperor of Japan and there is no disturbance of the Confucian ideal of an ordered society. The child serves the parent, the parent serves the governor, the governor serves the Emperor and the Emperor serves 上帝 Jōtei.

Another possible name for the Creator God is 天之御中主の神 Amenominakanushi no Kami. There are many difficulties with this name which render it unviable by itself. However, it may be possible to move from 上帝 Jōtei and identify His personal name in Japan as Amenominakanushi to overcome some of these challenges. At the very least, I think it is important for Christians, Japanese or not, to be aware of this aspect of Japanese history.

---

[6] Senkichiro Katsumata, *Kenkyusha's New Japanese-English Dictionary: An Entirely New Edition* (Tokyo: Kenkyusha Limited, 1954. Previous editions 1918 and 1951), 616.

Shintō: the Gospel's Gate

Amenominakanushi

As I wrote in part one, we can move from the identification of 上帝 Jōtei as the Creator God to the personal name of 天之御中主 Amenominakanushi in Japanese culture. While this name has been largely rejected by the current Christian body in Japan, it is vital that we follow Hiebert's four phases of critical contextualization: (1) learn the old beliefs and customs, (2) study them biblically, (3) evaluate them in the light of biblical teachings, and (4) create a new contextualized practice.[7]

Kato Genchi wrote briefly on the identity of 天之御中主の神 Amenominakanushi no Kami in *On Shintō*, referring to him as the "God of the Glorious Center of Heaven". We see places in Scripture that support this type of description of El Shaddai: Psalm 29:3 refers to YHWH as the God of Glory; Isaiah 6:2-3 the seraphim cry out that the earth is filled with YHWH's glory; and Ezekiel 1:26-28 offers a description of YHWH in His glory:

> [26] And from above the expanse that was above their heads there was the likeness of a throne, looking like a sapphire, and above the likeness of the throne was a likeness similar to the appearance of a human on it, but above it. [27] And I saw something like the outward appearance of amber, something like the appearance of fire, with a covering around it, from the likeness of his loins and upward. And from the likeness of his loins and downward I saw something like the appearance of fire, and it was radiant all around. [28] Like the appearance of a bow that is in the cloud on a rainy day, such was the radiance around it; thus was the appearance of the likeness of the glory of Yahweh. (LEB)

This is not how American Christians are familiar with thinking about YHWH because of the various artistic portrayals of Him. However, this Japanese description of the Creator God is supported by the Scriptural portrayal.

Along with 天之御中主の神 Amenominakanushi there appeared 高皇産霊神 *Takamimusubi* and 神結び *Kamimusubi*. Kato translates *Takamimusubi* as High Generative Power and 神結び *Kamimusubi* as August Generative

---

[7] Paul G. Hiebert, *Anthropological Insights for Missionaries* (Grand Rapids: Baker Book House, 1985), 186-190.

Power.[8] However, *Kami* is best understood as spirit and we can view 結び *Musubi* as Creative Power. Then 神結び *Kamimusubi* could be translated as Spirit of Creation. We could then understand 高皇産霊神 *Takamimusubi* as Word of Creation, that aspect of the Trinity which builds up (高) from nothing.

God Enthroned in Glory, Spirit of Creation, and Word of Creation easily correlates to the Hebrew understanding of YHWH, the Holy Spirit (Ruah Qodesh), and the Word of YHWH.

This translation may not be supported by the Ancient Japanese words. However, the Apostles took the Greek understanding of Theos, Pneuma, and Logos and gave them new meaning to fit the Hebrew understanding of El Shaddai. That is the same process that I am attempting to follow. The cultural understanding of 天之御中主 Amenominakanushi is hindered by the destruction of the Imperial Household in 645 A.D. when the residence and books were burnt to the ground.[9]

Another explanation of 天之御中主 Amenominakanushi is to be found in *Shintō: The Fountainhead of Japan* by Jean Herbert,

> An interesting detailed description of the Kami was given by Mr. Katsuhiko Kakehi, as follows: "1) Ame-no-minaka-nushi exists both in and above the empirical universe. He is both immanent and transcendent. He surrounds the visible world and partakes of its nature just as an outer enveloping circle or sphere includes but transcends a smaller concentric one. Thus dwelling above the phenomenal universe of human experience, he is yet a most intimate and inseparable part thereof. He possesses the attribute of *naka-ima* (or *doji-dosho*), "same time, same place", yet, although existing in all times and in all places, he is nevertheless superior to temporal and spatial limitations. (2) The designation *naka* (centre, or middle) in the name of this Kami is not to be taken as indicating localization in a central place in heaven (*ama*), in a physical spatial sense, but in the sense that all depends on him. (3) He is both *sosetsu* and *hisosetsu*, i.e. with reference to the phenomenal world, he is both creator and creation. In the work of creation he exhibits both and active and passive

---

[8] Genchi Kato, *Study of Shintō: the Religion of the Japanese Nation* (Tōkyō: The Zaidan-Hōjin-Meiji-Seitoku-Kinen-Gakkai, 1926), 66.

[9] Samuel Lee, *Rediscovering Japan, Reintroducing Christendom*, Kindle location 336 of 3457.

function. Life is not simply a force that creates, but also something created. (4) He is *fusho-fumetsu-fuzo-fugen*, without beginning, end, increase or decrease. He is the unfaltering basis and background of flux in the phenomenal world, transcending all change."[10]

It should be noted that the third point, "he is both creator and creation", has no reference to the kanji and contradicts point four which says, "He is without beginning, end, increase or decrease … transcending all change." Therefore, the third point seems to be an imposition of Shintō's worldview of spirit and matter spontaneously emerging from 結び *Musubi* to make the otherwise theistic understanding of 天之御中主 Amenominakanushi panentheistic.

Kakehi's explanation of 天之御中主 Amenominakanushi is nearly identical to the Christian formulation of monotheism, apart from the panentheistic formulation of his third point. 天之御中主 Amenominakanushi's name shows that he is immanent and transcendent, all that exists depends on him for existence, he is without beginning or end, and he does not change.

It is my hope that by examining the meaning of 上帝 Jōtei, 天之御中主の神 Amenominakanushi no Kami, 高皇産霊神 *Takamimusubi*, and 神結び *Kamimusubi* that the Church can better explain the Hebrew identity of El Shaddai. By doing so, we should be able to demonstrate that the Creator God is not a foreign, Western concept, but an idea that has existed in Japan since before the writing of the Kojiki.

---

[10] Jean Herbert, *Shintō: At the Fountain-head of Japan* (New York: Stein and Day Publishers, 1967), 238. Quoting Katsuhiko Kakehi, *Koshindo-taigi* (The Essentials of Old Shintō) (Tokyo, Shimizu-shoten, 1912), *Zoku-koShintō-taigi (vol. 2)*.

Shintō: the Gospel's Gate

CHAPTER 12: PSALM 51 PART 2

I began examining Psalm 51 in part one, focusing on the first strophe. We resume the study here by examining the second and third strophe.

As noted in part one, the second strophe is where David asks YHWH to cleanse his heart. Relationally and spiritually, this is the focus and highest point of tension of Psalm 51. A good word for it is fulcrum. Everything in Psalm 51 depends on the second strophe. Even David's life is focused here at this moment in his story.

One of the flags that this is the focus of the psalm is the reverse order of כָּבַס *kavas* wash and טָהֵר *taher* cleanse from verse 2 and verse 7. In verse 7, עָוֹן *awon* is replaced by חָטָא *chata*, both words expressing sin in Hebrew thought. This indicates that verse 2 and 7 have three terms in common and express the same plea. "My sin" תְּחַטְּאֵנִי *t'chat'eyni* disappears in the English translation, yet in the Hebrew, sin remains a separate thing from David, just as 'my car' or 'my pen' has ownership but the self is not interwoven with the object.

With the tension and resolution presented in the second strophe, it is surprising to me that more focus is not given to it in the Western church. Perhaps this is because the second strophe is speaking of cleansing David of his sin, so it does not fit into the Western guilt-innocence paradigm of forgiveness. Before commenting more and pursuing the answers to many questions, there are several elements that need to be examined.

Keywords

To reiterate, Psalm 51 is arranged into three strophes of five verses which have an interlocking pattern of the primary verb in Hebrew. In Psalm 51, the Hebrew words for sin appear a total of fourteen times: עָוֹן *awon* 4x, פֶּשַׁ

pesha 3x, and חָטָא *chata* 7x. However, טֻמְאָה *tumah* impurity is conspicuously missing from the entirety of the psalm.

There are three words that David employs to describe the solution to his sin: כָּבַס *kavas*, טָהֵר *taher*, and מָחָה *machah*. After defining these three keywords there will be an updated translation of Psalm 51 and then further comments and observations.

כָּבַס *kavas* occurs in Psalm 51:4 and 9 with the meaning of wash, and occurs fifty-one times in the Old Testament. One interesting thing is that the root word of כָּבַס *kavas* is כֶּבֶשׂ *keves* young ram or lamb, the difference being the final 's' sound represented by ס *samekh* and שׂ *sin*, respectively. An immediate question that appears is, "Is there a connection between a goat and washing?"

טָהֵר *taher* means to purify or to cleanse and is another of the words that David employs asking for YHWH to act upon him. טָהֵר is also used in the adjectival sense of clean, טָהוֹר *tahor* especially with describing animals, gold, and places. In Leviticus 20:25 טָהוֹר *tahor* appears as an antonym to טָמֵא *tahme*, which is an adjectival form of טֻמְאָה *tumah*, uncleanness or impurity.

מָחָה *machah* is a word that only appears twice in Psalm 51. From the Logos Bible Sense Lexicon, the form used here, מְחֵה *micheh*, is rendered in three possible ways: to blot out (wipe away, cover) or to forgive. Yet this very form is used with the object of a cloud in Isaiah 44:22. It would be quite ridiculous to speak of forgiving a cloud. In considering the meaning of the other two words, כָּבַס *kavas* wash and טָהֵר *taher* cleanse or purify, the sense of wipe away for מָחָה *machah* is in better keeping with the imagery being employed by David.

סָלַח *salach* forgive is conspicuously missing considering the focus of forgiveness in guilt-innocence Gospel presentations. Such an omission raises the question if forgiveness of sins is an appropriate understanding of the Gospel. If not, how should the Gospel message be conceived of in keeping with the Hebrew understanding of the solution?

Table 12.1 is an updated translation in light of the above word study. The reader will notice changes in column A and B.

Shintō: the Gospel's Gate

	A	B	C
1	¹Have mercy on me, Elohim. According to your faithful love and many mercies, **wipe away** my trespasses.	⁶ Behold your way delights the inward parts. You instruct me in wisdom.	¹¹ Do not cast me away from your presence. Do not take your Holy Spirit from me.
2	² Thoroughly **wash** me from my iniquity, purify me from my sin.	⁷ Purify my sin with hyssop, **wash** me white as snow.	¹² Return to me the joy of your salvation. Sustain me by your noble spirit.
3	³ Because my transgressions testify against me, my sin is always before me.	⁸ After you have crushed my bones, let me hear shouts of joy and gladness.	¹³ Then I will teach the transgressors your word. Those who have fallen away will return to you.
4	⁴ Against you alone I have sinned, entering evil before you. Therefore, you are righteous when you speak, pure in your judgment.	⁹ Remove my sin from before you, and all my iniquities **wipe away**.	¹⁴ Rescue me from [the curse of] bloodshed, Elohim, Mighty One of my Salvation, then my tongue will sing of your righteousness.
5	⁵ Behold, I have twisted authority and in sin the *mother* of *my* child conceived.	¹⁰ Purify my heart, restore the place of the Spirit of Elohim.	¹⁵ Open my lips, Lord, then *my mouth* will proclaim your praise.

Table 12.1 Updated Psalm 51

Observations

First, verse 7 is a reiteration of verse 2, with a change in the order of wash and cleanse. The phrase "my sin" disappears in the translation. Yet, David's focus is on the three different aspects of sin and he links them to impurity by asking to be cleansed or purified, washed, and wiped clean.[1] However, David does not mention the word for impurity, טֻמְאָה *tumah*. For all of his allusions to טֻמְאָה *tumah* why does he not use the word itself?

Second, the word מָחָה *machah* in verse 1 and 9 forms an inclusio (the use of a term or idea at the beginning and the end of a section[2]) around David's confession and his desired response from YHWH. It is as though David is presenting the antithesis to עָוֹן *awon*, פֶּשַׁע *pesha*, and חָטָא *chata* through the terms כָּבַס *kavas,* טָהֵר *taher*, and מָחָה *machah*. Which words corollate to which, I do not know.

One would expect טֻמְאָה *tumah* to correlate to טָהֵר *taher*, impurity to purify, and yet טֻמְאָה *tumah* is missing. Is there a word missing from the Hebrew understanding of the solution, making a total of four, just as there are four words describing sin?

Third, verse 7, תְּחַטְּאֵנִי בְאֵזוֹב וְאֶטְהָר, *t'chatani b'ezov w'et'har*, "purify my sin with hyssop," links David's imagery to the cleansing of people and a tent from death in Numbers 19:14-19, and the cleansing of leprosy in Leviticus 14:1-7. Although I used the imagery of spiritual cancer because of the phonetic relationship between טֻמְאָה *tumah* and tumor, David's imagery links the uncleanness to a type of spiritual leprosy and physical death. These two are linked since sin progressively eats away at the soul, searing it like a hot iron (1 Tim. 4:2), and leprosy is caused by a bacterial infection that eats away at nerves and other tissues.

---

[1] John Ayto, *Dictionary of Word Origins* (New York: Arcade Publishing, 1990), 421. "Pure traces to the Latin *purus* meaning clean and is the source of the words purify, purification, and purge."

The difference in English usage is that purify refers to removing contaminants from within a substance – air purifier, water purifier, etc – while cleanse is related to cleaning the surface of an object – hand cleanser, toilet bowl cleanser, etc.

[2] T. L. Jacobs, Virtue and Vice Lists, in *The Lexham Bible Dictionary,* ed. J. D. Barry, et al. (Bellingham, WA: Lexham Press), 2016.

Shintō: the Gospel's Gate

The rest of the sentence is "wash whiter than snow". A quite literal translation could be "My sin with hyssop purify and wash me whiter than snow." A more fluid English translation would be, "Purify my sin with hyssop and wash me whiter than snow." Sin is definitively linked to impurity and discoloration, while purity and whiteness is linked to righteousness by David's imagery.

Fourth is the issue of the second stanza. Originally, I wrote that the second stanza was an interruption of the first and third stanza. After further study, this initial impression is very insightful. The Western mind does not think in terms of purification and cleansing of sin. Instead it thinks of forgiveness and then demands immediate action. We move straight from the first stanza to the third stanza with little or no time reflecting on how we have been changed by the Gospel. In many ways a legal Gospel is an external Gospel – we have been legally justified and how we feel or perceive ourselves should conform to that legal standing.

Yet David takes just as much time describing YHWH's cleansing of his sin – more even, when one considers verse 1 and 2 are also asking for YHWH's cleansing – than he does describing his sin. After studying Psalm 51 and seeing the inclusio of מָחָה *machah*, the strophes, the repeated first and third person endings, and the progression of the strophes laterally (testify, hear, teach), I am convinced that this is not a poem that David wrote in a few minutes. I would expect that David spent at least a week to several months composing Psalm 51, meditating especially on the second strophe.

These strophes have another theme linking them: time. The first strophe is past-tense, the second strophe is in the present-tense, and the third strophe is in the future-tense.

In my own experience and judging from Western theology, we are not comfortable with the idea of pausing, of meditating. Western culture is action oriented, especially for men who have been the majority of theologians and teachers. If we are not doing something intellectually or physically, we are wasting time. As such, when a person becomes a Christ-follower they are immediately pushed to start sharing the Gospel with their friends and family. The new believer becomes nothing but another project and a gear in the religious machine.

However, the future action of the third stanza is the result of having been cleansed. Verse 12 and 13 provide the action and consequence clause, "Return to me the joy of my salvation and then I will teach the transgressors." David's picture of salvation then is not the removal of YHWH's wrath – his house will be torn apart by fratricide in a few years – but in the cleansing of his heart from sin. In Hebrew, David says that he will tell of YHWH's salvation to the transgressors – people who have left YHWH's path just as he had. He will tell of YHWH's ability to cleanse the heart and restore them to relationship with the Holy Spirit.

In verse 14, David addresses YHWH as אֱלֹהִים אֱלֹהֵי תְּשׁוּעָתִי *elohim elochey t'shu'ati*, "Elohim, God of my Salvation". David's view of salvation is not a legal view, but a view of having been cleansed from impurity. It is because of the joy that David receives in being cleansed that he praises YHWH and tells the transgressors of YHWH's faithfulness. This is so far removed from the Western understanding of the Gospel, it almost seems like a different religion. A parallel verse, paraphrased, is Jeremiah 4:14 where YHWH declares, "Cleanse your heart from wickedness, O Jerusalem, so that you may be saved." (LEB)

An early hurdle for my research is the confrontation that Western theology has forced the Bible to conform to Western cultural assumptions. The Bible is to influence our lives and our thinking, and yet the complete opposite approach has been followed. Western priority on guilt and innocence has overshadowed the Biblical priority of purity and impurity, shame and honor. How does David's view of salvation and sin relate to the Gospel? Can this provide a key – or perhaps *the* key – to reaching the Japanese? What is David pointing to with his imagery of salvation?

Chapter 13: Yom Kippur

Leviticus 16 introduces the festival of Yom Kippur. It is a passage generally understudied and benefits from analysis.

```
:1 Time Reference
:2-3 Instruction
    :4, 5 Preparation
        :11-15 Sin Offerings
            :12-14, 18 Altars
                :16, 19 Kippur
                    :20 Live Goat
                :21, 22 Confess
            :23, 24 Linen Clothes
        :27 Dispose of Sin Offerings
    :29 Tenth Day of Seventh Month
    :30 Cleanse from Sin
        :32-33 Make Atonement
:31 Instruction
```
Table 13.1 Yom Kippur Flow Chart

Leviticus 16:1 provides a time reference to being after Aaron's two sons died for approaching YHWH in an inappropriate manner, recounted in Leviticus 10:1-3. In verse 2, YHWH tells Aaron, through Moses, that he is not to come into the Holy of Holies as he desires, or he will die. It is as though YHWH is reminding us that the priests serve under strict requirements to treat the tabernacle as especially holy.

Verses 3 through 10 is a description of the preparation for the rite and the purpose of the sacrifices. In verse 3, Aaron is told to prepare a bull as a sin offering and a ram as a burnt offering. In verse 4, Aaron is instructed to wash himself and then put on a special linen tunic and turban. In verse 5, Aaron is instructed to select two male goats as a sin offering and a ram as a burnt offering from the congregation.

Verse 6 explains that Aaron will present the bull as a sin offering for himself and his household. The word for offering, וְהִקְרִיב *qariv* is in a hiphil form with a joining wav. The joining wav is rendered in several ways in the translations. Some use a sequential "then", others render it as "and", while others do not render it at all. But context and the hiphil form show that this is an explanation and should be rendered *"will* offer" in a future-tense command form joined with an explanative summary of the bull's purpose.

Verses 7 through 10 deals with the selection of the two goats, one being designated with a lot for YHWH and the other with a lot for Azazel. The goat who received the lot for YHWH is designated "will be offered", that is slain, as a sin offering. Meanwhile the goat whose lot was for Azazel is to receive atonement (כִּפּוּר *kippur*) and be kept alive before YHWH to be sent out into the wilderness "to Azazel".

Leviticus 16 moves into the actions of Yom Kippur with verse 11, which reminds the reader that the bull is for Aaron's sins. In verse 12, Aaron is told to take blood of the bull, two handfuls of incense, and a firepan into the Holy of Holies. That is, he moves from the place where the bull was slaughtered, into the Tabernacle, and then into the Holy of Holies through the separating veil.

While inside the Holy of Holies the incense is burnt so the smell and cloud of smoke fills the Holy of Holies (verse 13). Then in verse 14 Aaron is instructed to sprinkle the bull's blood seven times on the eastern side and the front of the Ark of the Covenant. In verse 15 and 16, Aaron exits the Tabernacle and slaughters the goat whose lot was for YHWH and repeats the process of sprinkling blood onto the Ark of the Covenant, just as he had done with the bull's blood.

There is a transition at verse 17, which makes special note that no one is to be in the Tent of Meeting while Aaron is making כִּפּוּר *kippur* of the Holy of Holies. In verse 18 and 19, Aaron is told to take a mixture of blood from the bull and the goat and spread some of the blood with his finger upon the Altar of the Lord, where the normal daily sacrifices were burned. Verse 19 explains that by doing this, Aaron will cleanse (טָהֵר *tahar*) the altar and make it holy

(וְקִדְּשׁוֹ v'qid'so) from the impurity (מִטֻּמְאֹת mitumoth from טֻמְאָה tumah) of the Children of Israel.

In verse 20, there is once again a transition. The act of cleansing the Tabernacle and the Tent of Meeting has been accomplished, and Aaron offers the live goat, whose lot fell for Azazel. Aaron places both of his hands on the head of the live goat and confesses over it all of Israel's עָוֹן ayon, פֶּשַׁע peshah, חָטָא chata, and טֻמְאָה tumah, that is, their twisting, transgressions, separation, and impurity, laying these things upon the head of the live goat.

In 16:22 the live goat, which carries the iniquities of Israel upon itself, is led away by a second man and is released into the wilderness to Azazel (:26). The singular use of עָוֹן ayon iniquity here is an example of synecdoche where one part is named to represent the whole.[1]

In verse 23, Aaron returns to the Tent of Meeting and takes off the linen turban and tunic, leaving the special clothing in the Tent of Meeting. In verse 24, Aaron washes himself, dresses in his regular clothes, and returns to the people, Aaron's reappearance from the Tent of Meeting signals the transition into the final phase of the Yom Kippur rite.

The two rams are offered as burnt offerings for sin. In verse 25 the fat from the bull and the goat are burnt on the altar. During this time, in verse 26, the second man, who released the live goat into the wilderness, returns to the camp and washes himself and his clothes before rejoining the camp of Israel. Verse 27 instructs that the bull and the goat offered for sin offerings are taken outside the camp of Israel and burned, though this is not done by the High Priest. Verse 28 instructs the person who burns the bull and the goat to purify himself, just as the man who released the live goat had to. Here the rite of Yom Kippur ends.

However, in verse 29 through 31, YHWH emphasizes the scope, time, and purpose of the rite of Yom Kippur. Yom Kippur is a permanent regulation which is to be observed by all people residing in Israel, native and foreigner, on the tenth day of the seventh month. It is a day of humbling themselves before YHWH and not doing any work. It is the day when Israel will be טָהֵר taher cleansed from their sins before the Lord.

Because Aaron will one day die, YHWH instructs for Aaron's son to take up

---

[1] Robertson McQuilkin, *Understanding and Applying the Bible: Revised and Expanded* (Chicago: Moody Press, 2009), 200.

the duties of the High Priest on Yom Kippur. This genealogical charge is presented in verses 32 through 34.

The chapter concludes, "Just as YHWH had commanded Moses, so he did."

Observations

The structure of Leviticus 16 forms a chiasm, with the live goat forming the climax of the ceremony. Totally, there are five animals sacrificed as part of the rite of Yom Kippur: a bull and two goats as sin offerings, and two rams as burnt offerings. It should be noted especially that the two goats are introduced as one sin offering.

For those observing the rite, there is very little action. Israel would see the slaughtering of the bull, the High Priest entering the Tabernacle, then reemerging to slaughter the goat, and reentering the Tabernacle. The entire time that Aaron is inside the Tabernacle there is no action for Israel to observe. Considering the size of the Tabernacle and the intricacies of the purification by blood, this was probably a considerable amount of time.

Next, they would see the High Priest place his hands on the live goat and the goat being sent out into the wilderness. Finally, the two rams were sacrificed and burnt, along with the prescribed pieces of the bull and goat. Seeing the live goat carrying away the טֻמְאָה *tumah* impurities and חֲטָא *chata* sins of the community was the high point of the ritual.

It should also be noted that the man who leads the goat into the wilderness releases it alive. Although this seems like it would be a slow death, animals were able to survive in the wilderness, grazing on plants growing around rocks and the various trees and shrubs. Some animals can smell water from great distances, and a goat would probably be able to search out water in this way.

כִּפּוּר *kippur* in its various forms appears 16 times, making it one of two essential keyword to understand.[2] The second keyword is עֲזָאזֵל Azazel. We

---

[2] Interestingly, the Mercy Seat on top of the Ark of the Covenant is כַּפֹּרֶת *kappōret*, but is not included in the count for כָּפַר *kāpár*. This suggests that the proper understanding of the Mercy Seat needs to be drawn from the verb and noun forms of כָּפַר *kāpár*, which "mercy seat" does not fulfill. Indeed, the word itself is defined as "the performance of

will first examine the translation of כִּפּוּר *kippur* as atonement and then introduce issues with עֲזָאזֵל Azazel and its translation as scapegoat.

---

reconciliation; cover, lid" (Mitchel, L. A. (1984). *A Student's Vocabulary for Biblical Hebrew and Aramaic* (p. 32).) and yet is glossed into English as Mercy Seat, suggesting that this is where punishment is held back from the people.

Shintō: the Gospel's Gate

CHAPTER 14: YOM KIPPUR: WORD STUDY

Word studies are perhaps the most tedious portion of any biblical research. This next section looks into the history and meaning of theological and biblical words. Most lay readers will probably be inclined to skip this section, but I think it will prove very useful and even interesting to read. While scholarly word studies would include a full entry of where the words are used and their various meanings, this is intended to be accessible to lay people and useful to scholars. As such, the word studies will generally be briefer and less rigorous than in purely academic writing.

Atonement

The first word to be examined is atonement. Because of the complexity in the working and understanding of atonement, it will be examined in three steps. First, the modern Western understanding of atonement. Second, the history and origin of the word atonement itself. And last, a look at the biblical usage of the root word, כִּפּוּר *kippur*.

Atonement as Propitiation

The model of atonement in the West is based on propitiation, which speaks of the appeasement of an offended party—specifically the Christian God—from wrath or anger.[1] Ted Peters further explains,

> Sometimes called the "penal substitution" model, the Reformation understanding of atonement through an exchange is in large part a further development of Anselm's notion of satisfaction. Here, Christ assumes the

---

[1] J. H. Russell, "Expiation, Propitiation" in C. Brand, and others, eds., *Holman Illustrated Bible Dictionary* (Nashville: Holman Bible Publishers, 2003), 533.

penalty belonging to sinful humanity and in exchange bestows upon us his justice and his resurrected life.[2]

This model of atonement as penal substitution is known as propitiation. Propitiation is a means of placating or pacifying displeasure due to an offence; hence an atoning action directed toward God, in the process of effecting man's salvation.[3]

Tambasco clarifies that,

> in propitiation theology the animal dies in our place . . . so that atonement would mean appeasement through the death of the animal.[4]
>
> In the popular view derived in part from Anselm, redemption is often conceived as a price that Christ pays to God in order to save us . . . . It was this concept of redemption that became attached to atonement, which joined to a theory of sacrifice as penal substitution and led to much of the explanation of atonement.[5]

The idea of Jesus satisfying, or pacifying, 上帝 Jōtei's wrath was further developed over time, until the Reformation. Here, propitiation was further developed by John Calvin and Martin Luther. George Smeaton explains that, "because of Martin Luther's deep consciousness of guilt, he presented the Gospel as bearing the penalty of the law, which became the viewpoint of Reformation theology."[6] And so, "for a century the Lutheran Church discussed the doctrine of atonement with Justification as its sole merit."[7]

---

[2] Ted Peters, "Atonement and the Final Scapegoat," *Perspectives In Religious Studies* 19, no. 2 (1992), ATLA Religion Database with ATLASerials, EBSCOhost (accessed August 22, 2016), 169.

[3] Gabriel Oyedele Abe, "Redemption, Reconciliation, Propitiation: Salvation terms in an African Milieu," *Journal of Theology for Southern Africa* 95, (July 1996): 3-12. ATLA Religion Database with ATLASerials, EBSCOhost (accessed August 22, 2016), 6.

[4] Anthony Tambasco, *A Theology of Atonement and Paul's Vision of Christianity* (Collegeville: Liturgical Press, 1991), 69.

[5] 5. ibid., 112.

[6] George Smeaton, *The Doctrine of the Atonement According to the Apostles* (Winona Lake: Alpha Publications, 1979), 525.

Shintō: the Gospel's Gate

Steve Chalke writes,

> penal substitution rests largely on the work of nineteenth century American theologian Charles Hodge, who, building on the work of John Calvin's legal mind, argued that a righteous God is angry with sinners and demands justice.[8]

As we can see, the doctrine of propitiation was developed over a long period of time and has had many steps of articulation. The primary, initial proponents seem to have been Anselm, Martin Luther, John Calvin, and Charles Hodge.

Origin of Propitiation

One question that needs to be examined before moving on, is where the word propitiation originates from. Merriam Webster's College Dictionary says that propitiate comes from the Latin *propitiatus* originating in 1583 and means 'to gain or regain the favor or goodwill of [someone] and is a synonym with pacify.'[9] The original Greek word translated into Latin as propitiate is ἱλασμός *hilasmos*.

Walvoord informs us that, "*Hilasmos* could be fittingly rendered "propitiation" (c.f. the noun *hilastērion*, "propitiation," in Romans 3:25 and the verb *hilaskomai*, "to propitiate", in Luke 18:13 and Hebrews 2:7)."[10]

ἱλασμός *hilasmos* and ἱλαστήριον *hilastērion* come from the root word ἵλεως *hileōs*. In its seven forms ἵλεως *hileōs* occurs just 20 times in the New Testament. Their forms and translations are in table 14.1.

It is strange that a word that translates with some form of mercy or cheerful could also mean satisfying wrath. Perhaps the most striking translation is Mercy Seat, which takes us back to the Hebrew word כִּפּוּר *kippur*.

---

[7] ibid., 529.

[8] Steven Chalke, "Redemption of the Cross," in *The Atonement Debate*, ed. Derek Tidball, David Hilborn, and Justin Thacker (Grand Rapids: Zondervan, 2009), 37.

[9] Merriam-Webster, I. *Merriam-Webster's collegiate dictionary*, Eleventh ed. (Springfield: Merriam-Webster, Inc., 2003).

[10] J. F. Walvoord and R. B. Zuck, *The Bible Knowledge Commentary: An Exposition of the Scriptures Vol. 2* (Wheaton: Victor Books, 1985), 887.

In this brief analysis of propitiation, a few things stand out. Propitiation was developed within the context of the guilt-innocence culture of the Western half of the Roman Empire. Propitiation developed over time until Martin Luther, who used it to develop the doctrine of justification. Western understanding of sin and salvation are developed within this framework.

There are those who disagree with the translation of ἱλασμός *hilasmos* as propitiation. Walvoord refutes these naysayers, writing, "Some say the term

Greek	Transliteration	Translation
ἱλεως	ileōs	merciful; gracious
ἱλάσκομαι	hilaskomai	propitiate; conciliate
ἱλασμός	hilasmos	propitiation
ἱλαστήριον	hilastērion	mercy seat; place of propitiation
ἵλεως	hileōs	merciful; gracious
ἱλαρός	hilaros	cheerful
ἱλαρότης	hilarotēs	cheerfulness

Table 14.1 Hileos

is not the placating of God's wrath against sin, but rather is an "expiation" or "cleansing" of sin itself. But the linguistic evidence for this interpretation is not persuasive."[11] By linguistic evidence, I assume that Walvoord is referring to analysis of the Greek and Latin vocabulary. This has strong traces of theological syncretism, where the authors have an *a priori* commitment to a position and then translate the Hebrew and Greek to justify that assumption.

Fortunately, in addition to linguistic evidence, there is also cultural and thematic evidence of the Scriptures. That "[h]ilasmos could be fittingly rendered propitiation" leaves the door open that it could be translated in other ways as well. Perhaps the greatest error in Walvoord's argument is that the New Testament is Greek words with Hebrew thought, as Professor Don N. Howell, Jr. would remind his students.

In this vein, Gabriel Abe writes, "the idea of propitiation is not prominent in the OT. The word as a religious term expresses pagan conceptions of appeasing the deity, hence it is inappropriate to Yahwism."[12] Reading

---

[11] ibid.

[12] Gabriel Oyedele Abe, "Redemption, Reconciliation, Propitiation: Salvation terms in an

Shintō: the Gospel's Gate

Leviticus 16 reveals that there is never a mention of 上帝 Jōtei's wrath against Israel being removed by the live goat, yet this is the model of propitiation.

Anthony Tambasco argues,

> The popular view of atonement [as Christ taking our punishment] is not supported by Pauline theology. Paul does not talk about Christ appeasing God's anger as a penal substitute.[13]
>
> Propitiation has God as object, i.e., God as one to be placated because of sin. Expiation has God as subject and sin as object, i.e., God as the one who graciously acts to remove sin.[14]

In Yom Kippur the High Priest acts on behalf of the nation by transferring impurity to the scapegoat before it is led away into the wilderness. In both cases, the scapegoat acts sympathetically by carrying away the community's impurity.

Another important similarity is that the practitioners recognized that they were unable to achieve self-purification aside from transferring personal and communal impurity onto an individual. This should not be considered psychosomatic since the Yom Kippur rite was instituted by 上帝 Jōtei through His representative, Moses.

Through such a comparison the question arises as to why Yom Kippur is known as the Day of Atonement, rather than the Day of Purification? To answer this, we need to examine the history of the translation of כָּפוּר *kippur*.

Origin of Atonement

In the context of Yom Kippur, the highlight, or crescendo, of the ritual was when the High Priest placed his hands on the head of the live goat and confessed Israel's עָוֹן *ayon*, פֶּשַׁע *peshah*, חָטָא *chata*, and טֻמְאָה *tumah* over it. The ritual was done on behalf of Israel as a nation, so the result of the ritual needs to be framed as to its impact on Israel. Douglas Judisch traces the

---

African Milieu," 6.

[13] Anthony Tambasco, *A Theology of Atonement and Paul's Vision of Christianity*, 94.

[14] ibid, 70.

word "atonement" to 1611, with the translation of the KJV which combined "at" with "one" to refer to the creation of unity between two groups at variance with each other, [so that] "make atonement" was a synonym of "propitiate" and "conciliate."[15]

Ted Peters writes,

> The first we know of the use of the term [atonement]. In [Thomas Moore's] *History of Richard III* atonement means reconciliation, especially between disputing political parties. Anglican Bibles began to use atonement in the sixteenth and seventeenth centuries, meaning "expiation" and "reconciliation."[16]

The implication is that the translators did not know how to translate כִּפּוּר *kippur*, so they simply chose a word to hide their ignorance. Otherwise, they would have had to simply use a transliteration of כִּפּוּר *kippur* with a footnote reading, "term of unknown meaning."

When learning a foreign language and encountering a word that is unfamiliar, the language learner has four ways to deal with the new word. First, they can ignore it; Second, they can consult a resource; Third, they can examine the word and attempt to analyze it for the meaning; Fourth, the language learner can look at the surrounding context and make an informed theory about the meaning of the word.

Because כִּפּוּר *kippur* is a keyword, ignoring or simply making a guess is not an option, while consulting resources revealed an answer of "we do not know" covered by obfuscation. Therefore, it is wise to start by looking at the word itself to see if there are any clues. The Hebrew letters in the pre-Babylonian form of כִּפּוּר *kippur* represent hand, spread, and head. In context, this symbolizes the transfer of Israel's spiritual impurity onto the goat, which God explained would then be carried away by the goat.

Yet this is not the only place that כִּפּוּר *kippur* occurs. There is undoubtedly an act of transference taking place as the sins are "removed" from the Tabernacle and placed upon the head of the goat. An informed guess, then is

---

[15] Douglas Judisch, "Propitiation in the language and typology of the Old Testament." *Concordia Theological Quarterly* 48, no. 2-3 (April 1984): 221-243. ATLA Religion Database with ATLASerials, EBSCOhost (accessed August 22, 2016), 223.

[16] Ted Peters, "Atonement and the Final Scapegoat," 153.

that כִּפּוּר *kippur* has the linguistic range of remove, transfer, or cleanse.

Tambasco develops the picture of atonement as expiation, meaning the removal of sin for the reuniting of the person to the will of God.[17] He continues that,

> Paul begins [Romans 5:1-11] by saying that we have peace with God, using the term eirene which is a relational word and is a synonym for reconciliation. Eirene is a translation of the Hebrew term shalom and expresses wholeness or fulness of relationship.[18]

Douglas Judisch writes,

> Many contemporary scholars connect כפר kippur with the Syriac kephar (to wipe away) and the Akkadian kuppuru (wash away, erase). Biblical confirmation of this is sought in the use of כפר kippur in parallel with מנה mineh, blot out, wipe away (Jer. 18:23) . . . . This was the understanding of the King James translators who used atonement for כפר kippur in 70 of its 99 occurrences.[19]

Tambasco explains,

> Atonement means God acting and humanity's cooperation in reuniting humanity with God through his union in Christ . . . . In technical terminology this description of sacrifice as atonement is called expiation, meaning the removal of sin for the reuniting of the person to the will of God. Expiation has God as subject and sin as the object, i.e., God as the one who graciously acts to remove sin. The word "expiation" (hilesterion) is literally "the mercy seat," or "the place where sins are wiped out."[20]

Jacob Milgrom recognizes a parallel between חַטָּאת *chatath* (sin offering) and כִּפּוּר *kippur*. He writes that חַטָּאת *chatath* carries the meaning "to cleanse, to expurgate, decontaminate" (e.g., Ezekiel 43:22, 26; Ps. 51:9).[21] He writes

---

[17] Anthony Tambasco, *A Theology of Atonement and Paul's Vision of Christianity*, 70.

[18] ibid, 106.

[19] Douglas Judisch, "Propitiation in the language and typology of the Old Testament," 223.

[20] Anthony Tambasco, *A Theology of Atonement and Paul's Vision of Christianity*, 69, 70.

[21] Joseph Milgrom, *Leviticus 1-16: A New Translation with Introduction and Commentary*

later, "In the context of חַטָּאת chatath, כִּפּוּר kippur means 'purge' and nothing else."[22] Pictographically, the sin/separation חָטָא chata is joined to the ת tav, which in pre-Babylonian form was the picture of a cross. Such a pictograph seems to demonstrate that "sin is removed at the cross."

The explicit statement of purpose for Yom Kippur in verse 30 should be used to inform us of the meaning of כִּפּוּר kippur, since the actions must bring about the purpose. "For on this day you shall be cleansed from your sins."

Perhaps this is an example of becoming so focused on the problem that one fails to see the solution sitting on the table. To remove 上帝 Jōtei's wrath or to bring forgiveness does not fit the lexical context, nor does it fit the relational drama unfolding between YHWH and the people of Israel. Instead of Day of Atonement, Leviticus 16 should be labeled the Day of Purification.

Forgiven

One word paired with כִּפּוּר kippur in the daily sacrifices, where the person presenting the sacrifice is said to be forgiven is סָלַח sahlach which occurs 46 times in the Bible.[23] Jenni and Westermann note that "סָלַח slḥ is the only OT term for "to forgive"".[24]

> With 46 occurrences slḥ is not a frequent verb and it appears much less often than appropriate for the significance of the message of forgiveness in the OT. In fact, several roughly synonymous expressions parallel the specific slḥ. They refer to covering or atoning for sin (kpr pi.), removing it (nśʾ), letting it pass (ʿbr), wiping it out, washing it away, cleansing it, and forgetting it. These marked expressions, which, like slḥ, derive from cultic rites, contrast with isolated, independent fig. expressions. They speak of Yahweh removing sin (Psa 103:12) and throwing it behind his back (Isa 38:17) or into the depths of the

---

(Doubleday: New York, 1991), 253.

[22] ibid., 255.

[23] L. A. Mitchel, *Student's Guide for Biblical Hebrew and Aramaic* (Grand Rapids: Zondervan, 1984).

[24] E. Jenni and C. Westermann, *Theological Lexicon of the Old Testament* (Peabody: Hendrickson Publishers, 1997), 798.

sea (Mic 7:19).[25]

Given the infrequency of סָלַח *salach*, one must wonder if forgiveness is as important as Western theologians make it out to be. Jenni and Westermann list seven words used in conjunction with the cultic rites, yet each of these speak of removal or cleansing, not forgiveness.

Is it more reasonable to insist on communicating the biblical theme as forgiveness of sins, or to think that the translators placed their cultural priorities above a direct and plain reading of the Scriptures? One way to check is to ask if there is another reasonable translation which would be in harmony with the predominant theme of Scripture and still have good logic individually.

וְאֶת־הַשֵּׁנִי יַעֲשֶׂה עֹלָה כַּמִּשְׁפָּט וְכִפֶּר עָלָיו הַכֹּהֵן מֵחַטָּאתוֹ אֲשֶׁר־חָטָא וְנִסְלַח לוֹ Leviticus 5:10 is translated as, "The second bird he must prepare as a burnt offering according to the regulation, and the priest shall make atonement for him for his sin that he has [committed], and he shall be forgiven" (ESV). This describes one of the daily sin-sacrifices for atonement and concludes by stating what will happen as a result of the offering.

The end of the sentence uses the keywords priest, atone, sin, and forgive. Structurally, the emphasis is not on the person presenting the sacrifice, but upon the sin. Since חָטָא *chata,* כֹּהֵן *cohen*, and the man presenting the sacrifice are all masculine, the masculine Niphal (passive voice, completed action) signature of וְנִסְלַח *w'nislach* does not do much to help indicate if it is the sin or the man who is the passive recipient of סָלַח *salach*.

If the recipient of וְנִסְלַח *w'nislach* is the man, we could make a legitimate translation of "restored" or "cleansed". But because there are other words that mean cleansed, "restored" would be a better choice. If the recipient is sin, then we could make a legitimate substitute translation of וְנִסְלַח *w'nislach* as "removed". Considering the other seven words and their dealing with sin as something gotten rid of, like a stain or a burden, then the understanding that it is sin and its resultant impurity that is the recipient of וְנִסְלַח *w'nislach* makes the most linguistic sense.

In America, forgiveness is thought to carry the meaning of "to not hold against." Inserting this into a passage such as Lev. 5:10 renders, "the priest

---

[25] ibid., 798-799.

shall make atonement for him for the sin which he committed, and I will not hold it against him anymore." Such a structure leaves the one presenting the sacrifice still carrying his טֻמְאָה *tumah* impurity.

Isaiah 55:7 becomes the nonsense of "let the wicked not hold it against his way." Numbers 14:20-23 also becomes nonsense, where YHWH will not hold the sin of Israel against them yet will not allow them to enter the promised land. Indeed, YHWH's actions here show that he *is* holding the rebellion of Israel against them. Either YHWH is lying or forgive is an inappropriate translation of סָלַח *salach*.

My only conclusion can be that forgive is an inappropriate translation and that סָלַח *salach* should have the range of meaning of removed or restored, depending on if it is sin or a person being acted upon. In this way, the reason that סָלַח *salach* "appears much less often than appropriate for the significance of the message of forgiveness in the OT" is because it is not establishing a theme of forgiveness. Instead, it expresses a cleansing of sin which YH provides to the repentant.

CHAPTER 15: YOM KIPPUR: SCAPEGOAT

A second term for consideration in the rite of Yom Kippur is Azazel. Azazel only appears four times, all of which are in Leviticus 16. The debate over the meaning of Azazel has been long standing and has been shrouded in mystery at least since the Babylonian exile. The four primary theories for the meaning of Azazel are: the name of the goat, a specific place, a state of non-being, or the name of a demon.[1]

Of these four theories, only two truly deserve examination because of their historical prominence. The Scriptures never indicate a state of non-being or annihilation of the spirits of demons or humans, so this can be discarded on lack of scriptural support. The idea that Azazel is a place actually comes from the same source which teaches that Azazel is a demon, so their rebuttals are the same.

Scapegoat

Let us first examine the less burdensome rendering of Azazel as scapegoat, as a name for the live goat. Joseph Milgrom traces the word scapegoat to the KJV translators, who used it because they did not know how to translate Azazel.[2] This would place the word scapegoat originating in 1611, while other sources credit the word scapegoat to William Tyndale's

---

[1] W. A. Elwell and B. J. Beitzel, "Azazel," in *Baker Encyclopedia of the Bible* (Grand Rapids: Baker Book House, 1988), 237.

[2] Joseph Milgrom, *Leviticus 1-16*, 1018. As quoted by Yaw Adu-Gyamfi, "The Live Goat Ritual in Leviticus 16," *Scriptura (Online)* 112, (2013): 1-10, ATLA Religion Database with ATLASerials, EBSCOhost (accessed August 22, 2016), 7.

Also see Pinker, *A Goat to go to Azazel*, page 12.

translation of the Bible into English in 1530.[3]

The simplest argument against the proper understanding of Azazel as scapegoat comes from the direct reading of the Hebrew of verse 10.

וְהַשָּׂעִיר אֲשֶׁר עָלָה עָלָיו הַגּוֹרָל לַעֲזָאזֵל יָעֳמַד־חַי לִפְנֵי יְהוָה לְכַפֵּר עָלָיו לְשַׁלַּח אֹתוֹ לַעֲזָאזֵל הַמִּדְבָּרָה:

w hasair alayw'aser hagoralô·rāl' 'ā·lā(h)' lă 'ăzā(')·zēl' yā 'ŏmăḏ hǎy' li p̄enê' yhwh l k̠ăp·pēr' 'āl āyw', l 'ōṯ' šǎl·lǎḥ' hă miḏ·bā'·rā(h) lă 'ăzā(')·zēl'.

but the goat on which the lot fell for Azazel shall be presented alive before the Lord to make atonement over it, that it may be sent away into the wilderness to Azazel. (ESV with inline transliteration)

If we keep the translation with scapegoat for Azazel as the name for the live goat, it becomes obvious that the scapegoat is sent into the wilderness to the scapegoat. The only way to deal with this contradiction is to translate the particle לְ le as "like" in verse 10 and 26. This is a very subtle way to deal with this problem, which a reader of the translation remains unaware of. Yet verse 8 is a full parallelism, which demands that YHWH and Azazel are personal beings.[4] Roy Gane offers a clearer insight into the matter,

> Through the lot ceremony, one goat is designated "for YHWH" (i.e., "belonging to YHWH") and the other is "for Azazel" (i.e., "belonging to Azazel, v. 8). So YHWH and Azazel are legal parties capable of ownership.[5]
>
> Because YHWH is the authority who commands the Israelites to perform the ritual (vv. 1-2), it appears that Azazel is his enemy. Therefore, it is likely that Azazel is some kind of demon and that his presence in an uninhabited region represents the "extreme opposite of God's holy presence in the Holy of Holies."[6]

---

[3] Merriam-Webster Dictionary. Accessed 4/20/2018. https://www.merriam-webster.com/dictionary/scapegoat.

[4] W. Möller, "Azazel," in The International Standard Bible Encyclopedia, vol. 1–5, eds J. Orr, J. L. Nuelsen, E. Y. Mullins, and M. O. Evans (Chicago: The Howard-Severance Company, 1915), 343.

[5] Roy Gane, Cult and Character: Purification Offerings, Day of Atonement, and Theodicy (Indiana: Eisnbrauns, 2005), 249.

[6] ibid., 250-1.

Shintō: the Gospel's Gate

The above observations demonstrate that scapegoat is not a valid translation because of parallelism and the simple fact that the goat cannot be sent to itself. Which means that the identity of Azazel as a demon is plausible and is the only real understanding of Azazel put forth by biblical scholars.

A Demon

If Azazel is a demon and YHWH himself is commanding a sacrifice to him, then this presents two contradictions. The first contradiction is how an omnipotent creator can be unable to conquer one of his own creations? There are only two options: Azazel is a coequal creator, or YHWH is not omnipotent. The second contradiction is that in Leviticus 17:7 YHWH commands the Israelites not to offer sacrifices to demons.

Either way, if Azazel is a demon, it proves that YHWH has contradicted himself, is not omnipotent, and is not trustworthy. Therefore, the Christian and Jewish faiths should be abandoned. For Atheist and Muslim apologists, Leviticus 16:8 and 10 and 17:7 are opportune verses to argue against the reliability of the Bible. To refute Azazel is a demon and disprove a contradiction, we need to understand where this teaching comes from.

The origin of the teaching that Azazel is a demon traces back to 1 Enoch, where he appears as the leader of the fallen angels, which is adopted by later Jewish, Gnostic, and Islamic traditions.[7] Chronologically, the use of 1 Enoch to interpret Leviticus is problematic, since it was written some time during the 400 years of silence in between Malachi and the Gospels, nearly 1,000 years later in history. It may be because of Azazel's obscurity that the author of 1 Enoch cast Azazel as the leader of demons which then worked backwards into the interpretation of Leviticus 16.

During the 400 years of silence, Israel may have felt abandoned by YHWH and were searching for someone who could replace or take vengeance upon YHWH. The theory that Azazel is such a powerful demon that YHWH had to make peace offerings to him would then be very appealing.

---

[7] F. L. Cross, and E. A. Livingstone, editors, *The Oxford Dictionary of the Christian Church*, 3rd ed. rev. (New York: Oxford University Press, 2005), 141.

Those already inclined to sorcery would have latched onto the idea, since in some branches of sorcery the more a deity is worshiped, the stronger it becomes. The idea of some beginning to practice sorcery with Azazel as their champion is supported by Pinker, who notes that there are similarities to how Azazel is treated in 1 Enoch with demons in Akkadian magical and incantation texts.[8]

Most likely, the use of Azazel in incantations would have started as sorcerers and magicians were developing spells and invocational magic. As this practice grew in popularity, a story about Azazel as a leader of demons was developed. Eventually these stories were written down into the First Book of Enoch, which then circulated and slowly entered the general knowledge. Eventually the idea that Azazel was a demon became an accepted teaching because it was a plausible explanation where no explanation was previously available.

A Third Option

When I originally began researching Leviticus 16 and Yom Kippur, I developed a theory about Azazel. Following the steps for understanding an unknown word (see the discussion on Kippur) the question became, "What was the function of the goat?"

Hebrew names for YHWH are constructed to show some aspect of what YHWH does or His Character. Names for people are also sometimes chosen to reflect what YHWH has done in the parents' lives, or to remind the child of who YHWH is. Take for instance Elijah, El Yi Ja, My God is Ya.

The function of the live goat is to carry away the impurities of Israel. Effectively, the goat is exiled from the nation and it carries the impurities into the desert. The Hebrew for 'carry away' and 'send into exile' is אזב *azav*, while אל *el* is the Hebrew for god. One reason that Azazel is so difficult for Hebrew scholars to identify is because of the oddity of the spelling. If the two words were אזב *azav* and אל *el*, how can the *bet* ב going from the *v* sound to a *z* sound be accounted for?

In Hebrew there is a form of elision, or collision of sounds, where a 'weak'

---

[8] Aron Pinker, "A Goat to go to Azazel," *The Journal of Hebrew Scriptures* vol. 7, (2007) (accessed 1-16-18, http://www.jhsonline.org/Articles/article_69.pdf), 18.

letter, such as the י (y), ו (w), and נ (n) consonants can join the previous vowel or disappear into a dagesh marking. The phrase for this is 'compensatory shortening' since the number of consonants decrease, making the word shorter.

What if the normal spelling of Azazel should have been אזבאל *azavel*. The problem would be that the aleph א would have to receive a *schewa*, a vowel marking that looks like a colon, אְ. However, aleph א is a guttural letter, produced in the throat like the g in great. Such a letter requires vocalization and a schewa represents the consonant being produced without any sound. This makes it impossible for the aleph א to receive a silent schewa. Therefore, the aleph א switches places with the ב *bet*. To show this switch, the ב *bet* engages in compensatory shortening into a ז *zayin*, producing the z sound, leaving the א alef without any vowel markings.

The meaning of Azazel should then be understood as 'the god who removes our sin.' I contacted Dr. Benjamin Noonan of Columbia International University to share this new theory. His reply was understandably challenging, saying that I would have to be able to demonstrate 'compensatory shortening' through Hebrew literature.[9]

However, I believe that there is another way to demonstrate the reliability of this theory. A discipline known as typology. But first, we turn our attention to the Shintō rite of お祓い Oharai.

---

[9] E-mail correspondence, 11-19-16.

Shintō: the Gospel's Gate

Chapter 16: Oharai

In chapter 5 I developed the label of panenpolypneumism to describe the Shintō worldview. The source of the problem for Shintō is that people and kami stray from their creative potential and purpose through wrong action. These wrong actions are called 罪 *tsumi* and result in 穢れ *kegare*, or impurity.

To return the people and kami to their proper function, purification rites are required. These rites take place in daily prayer for purification, occasional acts of bodily purification called 禊ぎ *misogi,* and the various 祭り *matsuri* which are held throughout Japan. These 祭り *matsuri* vary in purpose and form by region and the kami being invoked.

Among all of these purification rites, the most important is お祓い *Oharai*, which is practiced at most 神社 *jinja* throughout Japan twice a year. This chapter will examine what お祓い *Oharai* is, its history, and its significance to the Japanese worldview.

Introduction to お祓い Oharai

Jean Herbert summarizes お祓い *Oharai*,

> *Harai* designates 'the purification ceremonies of Shintō; the removal of all sins, pollutions and disasters by praying to the gods; the return to a condition in which one can approach the gods, by purifying body and mind'. It is a 'transitive purification'.[1]

A special word for this removal of 罪 tsumi is

---

[1] Jean Herbert, *Shintō: At the Fountain-head of Japan* (New York: Stein and Day Publishers, 1967), 80.

Tsumihoroboshi 罪滅ぼし atonement for sins; amends; expiation; penance
罪滅ぼしの expiatory
罪滅ぼしため as an atonement for one's sin; in atonement for (=in expiation of) sins (=crimes)[2]

Because Shintō is a way by which people relate to the spirits, maintaining a state of purity is necessary for proper harmony between man and the spirits upon which they depend for protection and provision. "In ancient Shintō documents purity meant ritual purity; and impurity, uncleanness or pollution, is, as a rule, of a physical nature . . . If a person has, even by chance, [become unclean] his body must be purified with due ceremony."[3]

A list of 罪 *tsumi* was provided in chapter 6 and so will not be reproduced here. It is sufficient to reiterate that any action that disturbs the harmony of the society or causes blood to be shed is considered 罪 *tsumi* and 穢れ *kegare* is the resultant state of impurity, which is fundamentally related to stains, blood, and death.

In a culture where the population lived so closely together and in interdependence for mutual support, any disruption was a threat to the survival of the community. If an individual offended the kami, the entire community could suffer, so purification was a community endeavor.

W. G. Aston writes,

> Things displeasing to the Gods are called by the Japanese tsumi (guilt), and the avoidance of such things by their worshippers is called imi (avoidance). As Motoöri points out, the tsumi of Shintō comprises three distinct things, namely, uncleanness, sin or crime, and calamity . . . . Certain calamities are included among tsumi because they were looked upon as tokens of the displeasure of the Gods for some offence, known or unknown. All tsumi involved religious disabilities or punishments. Uncleanness holds a far more important place in Shintō than moral guilt.[4]

---

[2] Senkichiro Katsumata, ed., *Kenkyusha's New Japanese-English Dictionary: An Entirely New Edition* (Tokyo: Kenkyusha Limited, 1954. Previous editions 1918 and 1951).

[3] Kato Genchi, *A Study of Shintō: The Religion of the Japanese Nation* (Tokyo: Meiji Japan Society, 1926), 114.

[4] W. G. Aston, *Shintō: The Way of the Gods* (New York: Longmans, Green, and Co., 1905), 247, Project Gutenberg eBook.

Jean Herbert elaborates,

> Due warnings, tatari, may be given by a Kami when he is dissatisfied or angered at a man's words or conduct. They may take the shape of disasters, *wazawai* . . . such as strange phenomena, mysterious destructive happenings, unhappiness, or even sudden death.[5]

If the cause of calamity is 穢れ *kegare* – impurity, then the solution is purification. Corduon explains one differentiation between purity and guilt, "Ceremonial purity is concerned with avoiding contamination from contact with an unclean object or person. If a moral violation is unintentional, it may be excused. But ritual contamination is objective."[6]

Guilt is subjective and originates from an outside source. Impurity is objective and is attached to one's core self. For instance, spitting on the street in Singapore is a criminal offense. Someone from Singapore would feel guilty spitting on the ground in America, even though it is not illegal. But no matter where you are, falling in a mud puddle makes you dirty.

Kato Genchi relates that お祓い *Oharai* is best translated as Rite of the Great Purification and was performed twice a year, once in the summer and once in the winter.[7] One should bear in mind that "a *ritual* is a privileged activity system that is believed to carry out a transformation process involving interaction with a reality ordinarily inaccessible to the material domain."[8]

お祓い *Oharai* provides the means by which a person may continue to advance toward purity and realization of their creative potential. Benedict expresses a similar idea when she writes, "Human nature . . . only needs to cleanse the windows of its soul . . . . If it has allowed itself to become 'dirty,' impurities are readily removed and man's essential goodness shines forth

---

[5] Jean Herbert, *Shintō*, 78.

[6] Winfried Corduan, *Neighboring Faiths: a Christian Introduction to World Religions* (Downers Grove: Intervarsity Press, 1998), 122.

[7] Kato Genchi, *A Study of Shintō*, 98.

[8] Roy Gane, *Cult and Character: Purification Offerings, Day of Atonement, and Theodicy* (Indiana: Eisenbrauns, 2005), 15.

again."⁹

Ritual of Oharai

A Year in the Life of a Shintō Shrine provides a detailed description of the お祓い *Oharai* ritual. In summary, the ceremony starts with a ritual cleansing of the Shrine, it's courtyard, and the participants. Then, 人形 *hitogata* are distributed in envelopes to everyone present, which are then removed from envelopes and which the participant rubs upon his or her body, to collect their 穢れ *kegare*. Next, the 人形 *hitogata* are placed back in the envelopes, collected by junior priests, and everyone proceeds to a special area of the shrine. Finally, a passage from the Norito is recited while the head priest throws the 人形 *hitogata* into a flowing body of water, which eventually carries the 穢れ *kegare* into the Land of Yomi, the underworld.[10]

Another account of お祓い *Oharai* comes from Karl Florenz's book titled *Ancient Japanese Rituals*. He indicates that お祓い *Oharai* was established as a twice-a-year ritual in 701 A.D.[11] with the earliest record being in 200 A.D.[12] An opening statement given by the officiating priest announces the intent to rid the officials, priests, and people of their 罪 *tsumi* and transgressions, called *toga*.[13] Florenz goes on in great detail:

> [the お祓い Oharai] ceremony performed at the *Sumiyoshi-jinja*, situated on

---

[9] Ruth Benedict, *Chrysanthemum and the Sword* (Rutland: Charles E. Tuttle & Co., 1976), 191.

[10] John K. Nelson, *A Year in the Life of a Shintō Shrine* (Seattle: University of Washington Press, 1996), 106-111.

[11] Karl Florenz and Ernest Mason Satow, *Ancient Japanese Rituals and the Revival of Pure Shintō*, Kegan Paul Japan Library (Unnumbered) (New York: Columbia University Press, 2002), 11. Accessed from University of Oregon Library 01-10-17.

[12] ibid., 9.
[13] ibid., 20.
I am not certain of the kanji. Wwwjdic suggested 咎 or 科 in a search for Romanized "toga" on 7-19-18.

the small island Tsukuda-shima in the mouth of the river Sumida-gawa, at Tokyo. This Shintō shrine, which is a branch shrine of the famous Sumiyoshi-jinja of Osaka, is one of the few shrines in the country, where . . . the ceremony is performed exactly in the same way as in the middle-ages . . ..[14]

Then the *Norito-shi* announces to the people his intention of performing the *Harahe*. The people utter their consent (lit. say "yes," which means that they are ready). The Norito-shi says: *Kore no-yu-niha ni ugonohareru hito mina ga ayamachi-okashikemu kusagusa no tsumi-goto wo harahe-do no oho-kamitachi umi-kaha ni mochi-idete Ne no kuni Soko no Kuni ni ibuki-hanachi sasurahi ushinahitemu. Kaku ushinaihiteba kefu yori hajimete tsumi to ifu tsumi wa araji to harahi-tamahi kiyome tamafu koto no Yoshi wo moro-moro kikoshimese to noru.*

Ie. "The great gods of the purification-place will take out into the river and sea all sorts of offences, that may have been committed either inadvertently or deliberately, by the people assembled in this pure courtyard, and blow them away and completely banish them and get rid of them into Hades[15]. Hear you all the circumstance (*Yoshi*) of the purification [which is performed with the intention] that from to-day there will be no longer any offence which is called offence, after they have thus got rid of them." . . . .

Then the *Norito-shi* recites the *Oho-harahe no kotoba* (our present ritual).[16]

After the recitation of this announcement the *Harahe-tsu-mono* are taken in a boat and thrown into the sea.[17] These *Harahe-tsu-mono* are described thus:

Towards the 25th or 26th of June (or December) the parishioners and other believers who wish to be purified go to the shrine and get from its official a so-called *kata-shiro* (形代), i.e. a white paper cut in the shape of a human garment. On this the person to be purified, writes the year and month of his birth, and his sex; then he rubs the paper over his whole body, and breathes his breath on it, by which procedure his sins are transferred to it, and takes it

---

[14] ibid., 28.

[15] ibid., 43. Note 80, page 108: Hades, generally called *Yomi-tsu-kuni* or *Yomo-stu-kani*, is meant. The translation "Bottom-Country" gives the meaning of the Chinese characters. . . ..

[16] ibid., 43-44.

[17] ibid., 44-45.

back to the shrine before the beginning of the ceremony. It is therefore also called *nade-mono* stroke-thing . . . . All the *kata-shiro* brought back are packed into two *ashi-dzutsu* "reed-sheath" which are placed on a table of black wood (*Kuroki no tsukuwe*), and are called *harahe tsu-mono* "purification-offering."[18]

The 人形 *hitogata* referred to above are a central element to お祓い *Oharai*. They are also known as 形代 *katashiro* "form-substitute", 撫物 *nademono* "thing for rubbing",[19] and 贖物 *agamono* "ransom"[20]. These paper dolls are in the form of a person wearing a kimono stretched out for storage. W. G. Aston writes,

> The principle of ransom is illustrated in the present day by the custom of kata-shiro (form-token) or nade-mono (rub-thing) . . . . believers who wish to be purified go to the shrine and obtain from its official a katashiro, that is, a white paper cut into the shape of a garment. On this the person to be purified writes the year and month of his birth and his or her sex, and rubs it over his whole body. When he has thus transferred his impurities to the paper he returns it to the shrine.[21]

The dolls are then gathered by the priests and destroyed by being thrown into water or by burning, depending on the time of year. In such a way, the doll and its 穢れ *kegare* are destroyed, leaving the individual and the community in a state of purity.

Kato Genchi elaborates that these dolls can be thought of as a ransom or an inanimate scapegoat.[22] The names of these dolls as 人形 *hitogata* and 形代 *katashiro* are instructive. Both contain the 形 kanji which translates as 'form'. Both also contain a character for person: 人 in 人形 *hitogata* and イ in 代 *katashiro*.

As Florenz demonstrates, it seems that the 形代 *katashiro* are called 撫物 *nademono* after the 罪 *tsumi* and 穢れ *kegare* have been transferred onto

---

[18] ibid., 26-27.

[19] W. G. Aston, *Shintō: The Way of the Gods*, 263.

[20] Kato Genchi, *A Study of Shintō*, 115.

[21] W. G. Aston, *Shintō: The Way of the Gods*, 263.
[22] Kato Genchi, A Study of Shintō, 115.

them, so that they function as sin bearers.

An important implication of お祓い Oharai is that the Japanese must admit that they have committed 罪 tsumi sin and have 穢れ kegare, impurity. Admission alone is not enough for them, the 穢れ kegare must be removed so that their relationship to the 神 kami and their creative potential can be restored. The cleansing takes a special form as the 穢れ kegare is transferred to the 形代 katashiro and then carried away.

穢れ kegare, then, is thought of as being something that gets attached to them, and under the proper rituals, can be removed. It is not a reflection on the moral character of the practitioner because even the best person will suffer from the effects of 穢れ kegare. In trying to find the ideal state of being, cleansing is essential to allow them to move forward in relationship with each other, the land, and the 神 kami.

It is possible that in the worldview of the Shintō practitioner that they are also affected by the 罪 tsumi or ill will of their ancestor 神 kami. They then stand as representatives for the dead, helping to transfer the 穢れ kegare of their deceased relatives, thereby helping them progress from death to reintegration with 結び musubi. One who refuses to be a conduit for their ancestors' progression is seen as committing a terrible act of betrayal and abandonment.

Figure 16.1 Agamono

By implication, those who do not observe the proper rituals, such as お祓い Oharai, invite disasters and misfortune upon themselves and their community. Such people are the source of problems and are guilty of breaking 和 wa, harmony, for the entire community.

Lafcadio Hearn offers further insight into the お祓い Oharai ceremony. He writes,

> From the earliest period Shintō exacted scrupulous cleanliness —indeed, we might say that it regarded physical impurity as identical with moral impurity, and intolerable to the gods. It has always been, and still remains, a religion of ablutions. The Japanese love of cleanliness—indicated by the universal practice of daily bathing, and by the irreproachable condition of their homes has been

maintained, and was probably initiated, by their religion . . ..

And besides the great periodical ceremonies of purification, a multitude of minor lustrations were exacted by the cult. This was the case also, it will be remembered in the early Greek and Roman civilizations—the citizen had to submit to purification upon almost every important occasion of existence.[23]

Purity of heart is not less insisted upon than physical purity; and the great rite of lustration, performed every six months, is of course a moral purification.[24]

Each Shintō parish-temple furnishes to all its Ujiko, or parishioners, small paper-cuttings called hitogata ("mankind-shapes"), representing figures of men, women, and children as in silhouette, —only that the paper is white, and folded curiously. Each household receives a number of hitogata corresponding to the number of its members,—"men-shapes" for the men and boys, "women-shapes" for the women and girls. Each person in the house touches his head, face, limbs, and body with one of these hitogata; repeating the while a Shintō invocation, and praying that any misfortune or sickness incurred by reason of offences involuntarily committed against the gods (for in Shintō belief sickness and misfortune are divine punishments) may be mercifully taken away. Upon each hitogata is then written the age and sex (not the name) of the person for whom it was furnished; and when this has been done, all are returned to the parish-temple, and there burnt, with rites of purification.[25]

. . .. The use of the hitogata, on which the name is not written, but only the sex and age of the worshipper, is probably modern, and of Chinese origin.[26]

Here, Lafcadio makes a definite statement of the relationship between moral and physical purity, in contrast with Kato Genchi's comment at the opening of this chapter. One explanation is that Lafcadio was writing during the Meiji period and Kato Genchi was writing at least twenty years later.

---

[23] Lafcadio Hearn, *Japan: an Attempt at Interpretation* (A Public Domain Book, 1907), 139-140, Kindle location 1340 of 4821.

[24] ibid., 140, Kindle location 1340 of 4821.

[25] ibid., 141-142, Kindle location 1356 of 4821.

[26] ibid., 142-143, Kindle location 1372 of 4821.
See also W. G. Aston, *Shintō: The Way of the Gods* (New York, Longmans, Green, and Co., 1905) Kindle Locations 3115-3116, "Confucius condemned the practice of offering effigies of men on funeral occasions because he thought it led to the substitution of living victims."

Shintō: the Gospel's Gate

An item of importance is Lafcadio's depiction of how Shintō morals and customs were enforced upon the Japanese people. Although Shintō has no written moral documents, the moral expectations of Shintō were as real and present to the Japanese as the very wind upon their faces, and any breach was dealt with, sometimes harshly. Brief quotes do not suffice in explaining this reality of the Japanese, so I can only recommend that the reader also read *Japan: An Attempt at Interpretation* especially chapters 4 – 6.

Another important item is Lafcadio's estimation that the 人形 *hitogata* is of Chinese origin, which has some very interesting implications. Firstly, what was used prior to the 人形 *hitogata* for the removal of 罪 *tsumi* and 穢れ *kegare* from the community? Secondly, if the 人形 *hitogata* did come from China, it will be of immense value if a scholar of Chinese religions is able to demonstrate when, how, and why these paper dolls were used. Were they of Taoist origin or from the worship of 上帝 ShangDi? Thirdly, could these 人形 *hitogata* have also been introduced to other Asian countries, such as Thailand, Vietnam, and Korea through China as well?

Reflections

Shintō is a spiritual practice concerned with maintaining and promoting the harmonious development of the world. The physical world is dependent upon and is a manifestation of the spiritual world. At the center of Shintō is the expiatory rite of お祓い Oharai wherein the 罪 *tsumi* and 穢れ *kegare* of the community can be removed and harmony with the 神 *kami* restored.

When I received 人形 *hitogata* from the shrine 出雲大社美作分院 *Izumo Taisha Meizu Branch* in Tsuyama-shi, Okayama-ken in the spring of 2017, I was surprised that it had six silhouettes on one long piece of paper. It is from these 人形 *hitogata* that I designed figure 16.1. Based on descriptions from quoted authors, shrines use various 人形 *hitogata* designs for お祓い Oharai.

The central figure of お祓い Oharai is the 形代 *katashiro* or 人形 *hitogata* which is used to carry away the 罪 *tsumi* and 穢れ *kegare* of the participants. These paper dolls are also referred to as substitutes – substitutes of the person being cleansed or for blood sacrifice? The next chapter will examine that question.

Shintō: the Gospel's Gate

Chapter 17 Shintō Sacrifice

As an outsider it is difficult to understand how a piece of paper can take on the 穢れ *kegare* of a living person and carry it away. It is therefore necessary to ask after the identity and origin of the 形代 *katashiro*, also called a scapegoat. W. G. Aston relates that the 形代 *katashiro* (form-token) illustrates the principle of ransom.[1]

In my opinion, it is a strong possibility that the 形代 *katashiro* or 贖物 *agamono* is so named as a replacement for a human victim who was killed to cleanse the village, clan, or city. Aston observes, "The more intimately the objects offered are connected with the person of the offender, the more effectual is the sacrifice."[2] This adds to the possibility of human sacrifice since a piece of paper cannot be more or less connected to a participant. If human sacrifice existed at one time in Shintō it should be supported through the Japanese language, other rites, and archeological discoveries. As a case in point, in the Japanese language, the word for human sacrifice is 人身御供 *hitomigokuu*, with the act itself being 人身御供上げる *hitomigokuuageru*.[3]

Discussions of human sacrifice in Shintō are generally prefaced with words like "legendary" and "supposed" giving it an appearance of speculation that has not been established by historical accounts or archaeology. It would be surprising if Shintō did not use human sacrifice at some point in its history, given its nearly universal appearance in cultures

---

[1] W. G. Aston, *Shintō: The Way of the Gods* (New York: Longmans, Green, and Co., 1905, Project Gutenberg eBook, 2014), 262.

[2] ibid., 262.

[3] Senkichiro Katsumata, ed., *Kenkyusha's New Japanese-English Diction: An Entirely New Edition* (Tokyo: Kenkyusha Limited, 1954. Previously editions 1918 and 1951), 447.

An Honorable Death

The first form of human sacrifice we will examine is a form of self-sacrifice. The most common form of it was performed in crisis but it also had a ritual expression. This form of sacrifice is simultaneously celebrated and taboo within Japanese culture. 切腹 Seppuku.

Nigel Davies observes,

> For the Japanese, seppuku has a special mystery since it is tied to the ancient notion that the mind exists in the stomach. Therefore in committing seppuku a man is purging his sins and dying at the same time . . . .. As long as the proper ritual was observed, the deed was in every sense a religious sacrifice, whether self-inflicted or imposed from above, and the same word served for both varieties.[4]

Stephen Turnbull elaborates further on the samurai's view of 切腹 seppuku, writing,

> In the world of the warrior, seppuku was a deed of bravery that was admirable in a samurai who knew he was defeated, disgraced, or mortally wounded. It meant that he could end his days with his transgressions wiped away and with his reputation not merely intact but actually enhanced.[5]

Although seppuku itself may not be seen today, the idea that a Japanese person may kill themselves to cleanse themselves and their families from disgrace is not absent. The idea of suicide being used to 'make amends' or to express true remorse is not unique to Japan. It is also seen in China and the United States, though it is doubtful anyone keeps records to show how many suicides are attributed to a need to cleanse oneself of misdeeds or shame.

Benedict writes, "the Japanese love the theme [of seppuku]. They play up

---

[4] Nigel Davies, *Human Sacrifice: In History and Today* (New York: Morrow, 1981), 126, 128.

[5] Stephen Turnbull, *Samurai – the World of the Warrior* (Oxford: Osprey Publishing Ltd., 2003), 42.

suicide as Americans play up crime and they have the same vicarious enjoyment of it."[6] To give an accurate picture, Benedict comments elsewhere, "they repudiate the idea that they are sacrificing themselves . . . . the Japanese speak, instead, of 'voluntary' death . . .. Such a voluntary death, they say, achieves an object you yourself desire."[7] What is this object that the samurai desired so much that they were willing to die?

> Sacrifice brings not only unity but purification and renewal. This renewal is often symbolized by ritual bathing or baptism, for resurrection finds its roots in the unclean; it is born of sin, which must be washed away . . . .. The Japanese Samurai committed seppuku to make amends for wrongs that dishonoured the community.[8]

Hitobashira

Kato Genchi provides accounts of human and animal sacrifices on pages 103-107 in *A Study of Shintō: The Religion of the Japanese Nation*. Among these accounts is a report of a Catholic missionary who witnessed a samurai and his retainers who sacrificed themselves under the foundation stones of a castle to become the guardian spirit of the castle.[9]

However, he does not indicate the date or location of this event, so we are left to wonder if this took place in Meiji Japan or Tokugawa Japan. Such forms of human sacrifice were collectively referred to as 人柱 *hitobashira* a human sacrifice (=immolation)[10]. Although here referenced as immolation, drowning and live burial were also included, as demonstrated below.

Tsuda Noritake relates that the tradition of human sacrifice is also tied to

---

[6] Ruth Benedict, *Chrysanthemum and the Sword: Patterns of Japanese Life* (Rutland: Charles E. Tuttle & Co., 1976), 168.

[7] ibid., 289.

[8] Nigel Davies, *Human Sacrifice: In History and Today*, 275.

[9] Kato Genchi, *A Study of Shintō: The Religion of the Japanese Nation* (Tōkyō, Japan: The Zaidan-Hōjin-Meiji-Seitoku-Kinen-Gakkai (Meiji Japan Society), 1926), 105.

[10] Senkichiro Katsumata, *Kenkyusha's New Japanese-English Dictionary*, 447.

the building of large bridges. A diary from the 15th century recounts a woman and her child who were sacrificed at a bridge being built over the Nagara River, referred to as Nagara no Hitobashira.[11] W. G. Aston also relates that 人柱 hitobashira were buried alive in the foundations of bridges, castles, and artificial islands.[12] Elsewhere, there is a report,

> Every local province has some stories to tell of noble martyrs who offered themselves to be buried alive as *hito-bashira* or human-sacrifice for the sake of their fellow-creatures. When a great difficulty was met in the construction of a bridge, castle, embankment or anything else that was related to a river or a sea, it was attributed to the anger or displeasure of the water-god, and a living person was offered to appease the angry deity. The victim was buried alive under the foundation of the construction as a *hito-bashira*.
>
> The earliest "human-post" recorded in the history of Japan was offered to the river deity of the River Yodo in 324 A. D. . . . . When a few years ago they repaired the Nijy-Bashi, which is the front entrance to the Imperial Palace, Tokyo, they found some dozen human bodies buried there, some in a standing position and others lying . . . . The bridge being the front entrance of the Imperial Palace and originally of the Shogunate Palace in feudal days, is the last place for a dead body to be buried, so some orthodox Japanese were of the opinion that these bodies had been buried as human sacrifices.[13]

Kato Genchi provides a grim summary, "accounts of the living being buried alive, which in Japanese history are so numerous . . . ."[14] In speaking of 人柱 hitobashira, Noritake Tsuda writes,

> Therefore it is reasonable to assume that also in Japan this custom [of human sacrifice] should have been practiced once . . . . Where shall we find the origin of the traditions which we have characterized above? No scholar could give

---

[11] Noritake Tsuda, "Human Sacrifices in Japan," *The Open Court* vol. 1918, issue 12, Article 6, (12, 1918): 763, http://opensiuc.lib.siu.edu/ocj/vol1918/iss12/6. Last accessed 10/18/16.

[12] W. G. Aston, *Shintō: The Way of the Gods*, Kindle locations 3088-3092.

[13] H. S. K. Yamaguchi, *We Japanese* (Yokohama: Yamagata Press, 1937; reprint, Yokohama: Yamagata Press, 1950), 228-229 (page citations are to the reprint edition).

[14] Kato Genchi, *A Study of Shintō*, 42.

any definite answer to this question.

The custom, however, is also found in ancient China, for, as it is recorded in the *Ch'un Ts'ew,* with *Tso Chuen* compiled in the fifth century B.C., it must have been practiced in the remote ages of Chinese history.[15]

Another form of sacrifice is recounted by Lafcadio Hearn, the human hedge, performed as part of ancestor worship (the following quote is rather graphic, and some readers may wish to skip it altogether).

> At the funerals of great personages [human] sacrifices were common. Owing to beliefs of which all knowledge has been lost, these sacrifices assumed a character much more cruel than that of the immolations of the Greek Homeric epoch. The human victims were buried up to the neck in a circle about the grave, and thus left to perish under the beaks of birds and the teeth of wild beasts. The term applied to this form of immolation, — hitogaki, or "human hedge,"—implies a considerable number of victims in each case.[16]

Through this grisly overview, it seems to be well supported that human sacrifice was a feature of Shintō, even up through the 1900s via the practice of 切腹 *seppuku*. In the records of 人柱 *hitobashira*, people are sacrificed to appease the kami or to protect a site. A possibility arises that Shintō Shrines, or 神社 *jinja*, may have been dedicated to the kami through acts of human sacrifice.

お祓い Oharai and 人身御供 Hitomigoku

Yet to be addressed is the question of whether human sacrifice was ever part of the お祓い Oharai ceremonies. Karl Florenz provides one example where an affirmative answer is given:

> The fourth reference [to Oho-harahe], on the 30th day 7th month, 10th year (19th August, 681) runs : "Orders were given to the whole Empire to hold a *great Purification ceremony*. At this time each Kuni no Miyatsuko supplied as purification-offering one slave, and thus the purification was done."[17]

---

[15] Noritake Tsuda, "Human Sacrifices in Japan," 766.

[16] Lafcadio Hearn, *Japan: an Attempt at Interpretation* (A Public Domain Book, 1907), 37, Kindle location 335 of 4821.

It can be supposed that the slaves thus provided were either drowned or burned alive as 人身御供 hitomigoku. One can only imagine what these unfortunate people must have endured on the long walk to the site of the お祓い Oharai ceremony and then standing in line, watching as their fellows were killed one by one.

Another example of human sacrifice exists in addition to that of お祓い Oharai. Kato Genchi in *What is Shintō?* writes,

> The annual festival still observed at the Kō-no-Miya Shrine, dedicated to the Owari-ōkunitama or Local Guardian Spirit of Owari Province, reminds us of a Shintō cult of expiatory human sacrifice of olden times (a piacular rite), and exorcism inseparably connected therewith . . .. In remote antiquity, it is highly probable that the ceremony involved a real human victim.[18]

Directly opposite this text, on page 33, is a picture from *Owari-Meisho-Zue* which shows a man with four candles on his head being chased from a Shintō shrine by eight Shintō priests with drawn swords. The caption for this picture reads, "The human scapegoat with candles on his head in the Shintō ceremony of exorcism being chased from the Kōnomiya Shrine."

Plutschow elaborates,

> At Owari Ōkunitama shrine, Konomiya, Inazawa, Aichi prefecture, on lunar 1/13-14, a man is selected to take the role of recipient of all evil in the village. He is called Shinotoko or 'divine man'. Villagers touch him and he touches the villagers in an effort to receive into himself all evil that people might carry around, or which has attached itself to their person. After this, he must carry a big load of mud in the form of a rice cake on his back, indicating the weight of the evil and misfortune he has accumulated. The villagers then chase him out of the community. This ritual allegedly goes back about 1,200 years to the Nara period (710-784), when it was introduced as a response to an epidemic.[19]

---

[17] Karl Florenz and E. M. Satow, *Ancient Japanese Rituals and the Revival of Pure Shintō*, Kegan Paul Japan Library (Unnumbered) (New York: Columbia University Press, 2002), 11. Accessed from University of Oregon Library 01-10-17. Digitized by Google.

[18] Kato Genchi, *A Study of Shintō*, 153. See also Kato Genchi, *What is Shintō?* (Tokyo: Maruzen Company Ltd., 1935), 32. *Owari-Meisho-Zue* translates as Guide to Famous Owari Sites according to an internet search, so it may be Genchi's reference source.

[19] Herbert Plutschow, *Festivals of Japan* (Surrey: Japan Library, 1996), 18. Owari

Shintō: the Gospel's Gate

It should be noted that 神男 *shinotoko* could also be translated as 'god-man'.

An article about the Konomiya Hadaka Matsuri posted on the website Nagmag goes into greater detail about the festival as it is held currently. The man chosen as 神男 *shinotoko* is secluded in the shrine, where his hair is completely shaved off, and he undergoes purification ceremonies for three days. On the third day, around 3 p.m., he is removed from the shrine and the assembled crowd attempt to slap and grab the 神男 *shinotoko* to transfer their bad-luck onto him as he runs through the courtyard and tries to return to the safety of the shrine, a feat which has been known to take 30 minutes to two-hours. At 3 a.m. the next morning, the 神男 *shinotoko* is given a large ball of rice that has been rolled in the ashes of burnt offerings, representing the accumulated evil and bad luck, which he carries away and buries somewhere.[20]

The Hadaka Matsuri 裸祭り, or the Naked Man Festival, is so named because the participants, all men, wear nothing but a 褌 *fundoshi*, a type of loincloth. Being nearly naked, outside in the middle of winter, drunk, and surrounded other drunk men, seems to be a recipe for injuries and the risk of death. However, judging from the turnout of participants and the fact that the role of 神男 *shinotoko* is now voluntary, this festival is very well received and enthusiastically celebrated within Japan. The reason, it would seem, is because of the chance to get rid of one's 罪 *tsumi* and 穢れ *kegare*.

W. G. Aston informs us of another ritual almost identical to the one held at Konomiya Jinja, proving that it was not an isolated ritual:

> The principle of ransom is also illustrated by the following extract from the Shintō Miōmoku (1699): "At the festival of Nawoye, held at the shrine of Kokubu in the province of Owari on the 11th day of the 1st month, the Shintō priests go out to the highway with banners and seize a passer-by. They wash and purify him, and make him put on pure clothing. He is then brought before the God. A block, a wooden butcher's knife, and chopsticks for eating flesh are provided. Separately a figure is made to represent the captive. It is placed on

---

Ōkunitama and Konomiya Jinja are one and the same building. See the previous citation from Kato Genchi.

[20] Nagmag, Nagoya's Magazine, *Konomiya Hadaka Matsuri*, http://nagmag.jp/konomiya-hadaka-matsuri-february-28-2018. Posted May 25, 2018. Last accessed May 25, 2018.

the block with the captured man beside it, and both are offered before the God. They are left there for one night. The next morning the priests come and remove the man and the effigy. Then they take clay, and, making it into the shape of a rice-cake, place it on the captive's back, hang a string of copper cash about his neck, and drive him away. As he runs off, he is sure to fall down in a faint. But he soon comes to his senses. A mound is erected at the place where he falls down, and the clay rice-cake deposited on it with ceremonies which are kept a profound mystery by the priestly house. . . .[21]

Reflections

Ruth Benedict's assertion that "shame cultures do not provide for confessions . . . they have ceremonies for good luck rather than for expiation"[22] is only half correct.

Instead of trying to get rid of guilt, which is the mechanism of confession, Shintō attempts to get rid of shame and impurity through its most important expiatory rituals of お祓い Oharai, 切腹 seppuku, and various 祭り matsuri. What actions caused the impurity is of no consequence and is not addressed in modern お祓い Oharai, yet the practitioner must admit that they are impure to participate in the ritual. The luck which Benedict refers to is actually the resultant blessing from the 神 kami, received once the relationship is restored.

Kato Genchi's observations regarding the human scapegoat at Kōnomiya Shrine[23] and the evidence for human sacrifice lends weight to the idea that the 形 katashiro are substitutes for human sacrifice, rather than being an inanimate representation of the person being cleansed from 罪 tsumi and 穢れ kegare. Although human sacrifice is no longer used in Shintō, the reality remains that it was part of Shintō practice.

---

[21] W. G. Aston, *Shintō: The Way of the Gods*, Kindle locations 3099-3108.

[22] Ruth Benedict, Chrysanthemum and the Sword, 223.

[23] Kato Genchi, A Study of Shintō, 153.

CHAPTER 18 TYPOLOGY

There is a form of prophetic interpretation called typology which looks to see the people, events, places, and things of the Old Testament as representing spiritual realities and concepts found in the New Testament. "*Typological Interpretation* is specifically the interpretation of the Old Testament based on the fundamental theological unity of the two Testaments whereby something in the Old shadows, prefigures, adumbrates something in the New."[1] Three verses are of immediate help:

> Colossians 2:17 "Do not let anyone judge you in regard to food and drink or in the matter of a festival or a new moon or a Sabbath day. These are a shadow of what was to come; the substance is the Messiah."
> John 3:14 "As Moses lifted up the serpent in the wilderness, so must the Son of Man be lifted up that whoever believes in Him should not perish."
> Hebrews 8:5 "These serve as a copy and a shadow of the heavenly things, as Moses was warned when he was about to complete the tabernacle."

However, typology is regarded with a high degree of suspicion by many theologians. Primary among the detractors is Bishop Herbert Marsh "the ablest and most systematic expounder"[2] against allegorical interpretation, in which he included typology. Before a positive assertion of a typological interpretation can be made, the objections raised by Marsh need to be

---

[1] Bernard Ramm, *Protestant Biblical Interpretation: A Textbook of Hermeneutics*, 3rd rev. edition (Grand Rapids: Baker Books House, 1970), 223.
This chapter was originally written for RES 7961 in the spring of 2014 at CIU and titled "Esther in Light of the Gospel".

[2] Patrick Fairbairn, *Typology of Scripture, Two Volumes in One, b1* (Reprint; Grand Rapids: Kregel Publications, 1989), 19.

addressed.

Allegory

The term allegory is defined in two different ways, depending on its area of usage. In literary terminology, an allegory is a story where the characters and settings represent something else in a one-to-one correlation, ranging from every character and setting as in John Bunyan's *A Pilgrim's Progress*[3] to a semi-allegorical work where only certain characters and settings are intended to represent something else, such as C. S. Lewis's *Chronicles of Narnia*[4].

However, in the theological definition, allegory is a style of interpretation wherein any person, event, or object can be made to be a symbol of anything that the interpreter desires. Marsh explains,

> Now a Metaphor . . . is a kind of transfer, which takes place whenever a word, belonging properly to one subject is transferred to another subject to which it does not properly belong.[5]
>
> Allegory, according to its original and proper meaning, denotes a representation of another thing. Every Allegory therefore must be subjected to a two-fold examination: we must first examine the immediate representation, and then consider, what other representation it was intended to excite.[6]
>
> Now in most Allegories the immediate representation is made in the form of a narrative: and since it is the object of an Allegory to convey a moral, not an historic truth, the immediate representation is of no further value than as it leads to the ultimate representation.[7]

---

[3] John Bunyan's *A Pilgrim's Progress*, published in 1678, tells the story of Christian, who moves from the City of Destruction through various locations such as the Slough of Despond, until he comes at long last to the Celestial City, meeting characters such as Faithful along the way. It teaches theology through its characters and settings while simultaneously entertaining its readers.

[4] C. S. Lewis, *Chronicles of Narnia* (New York: Harper Collins Publishers, 1989).

[5] Herbert Marsh, *Lectures on the Criticism and Interpretation of the Bible* (London: J. Smith Printer to the University, 1828), Kindle Location 4015.

[6] ibid, Kindle location 4031.

Ramm clarifies,

> The Greek philosophers developed allegorical interpretation to deal with the fanciful, grotesque, absurd, and immoral sections of Homer and Hesiod. . . . Allegorical interpretation believes that beneath the letter (*rhete*) or the obvious (*phanera*) is the real meaning (*hyponoia*) of the passage. . . . [So allegory presumes] that the scripture has no foundation in fact, a mere myth or fabulous description invented for the sole purpose of exhibiting the mysteries of divine truth. . . .[8]

In light of this clarification, Marsh concludes that with allegorical interpretation "the meaning of Scripture will be involved in perfect ambiguity: it will assume as many different forms, as the fancies of interpreters."[9] By way of illustration Marsh relates a letter from Pope Innocent the Third to the Emperor of Constantinople, wherein the Pope explains how the creation of the sun and the moon in Genesis 1 represent the authority of the pope being greater than the authority of monarchs—an authority which he used to anoint and depose kings.[10]

Any proposed method of interpretation that does away with the authority of Scripture by declaring it to be mere fantasy is a method that is best quarantined, for "with such an arbitrary and elastic style of interpretation, there is nothing either false or true in doctrine, wise or unwise in practice, which might not claim support in scripture."[11]

The very fact that Scripture is a guide how to live a life that is pleasing to 上帝 Jōtei and to guide people into truth and life (Psalm 119:160; 2 Tim. 2:25-26) is swept away in a quest for "a higher truth," which sounds eerily similar to Lucifer's boast in Isaiah 14:13-14 by which is meant that he intended to become greater than his Creator and take 上帝 Jōtei's glory for

---

[7] ibid, Kindle location 4035.

[8] Bernard Ramm, *Protestant Biblical Interpretation*, 25.

[9] Herbert Marsh, *Lectures on the Criticism and Interpretation and Interpretation of the Bible*, Kindle location 4322.

[10] ibid, Kindle location 4428.

[11] Bernard Ramm, *Protestant Biblical Interpretation*, 5.

himself.

Allegorical Typology

Fairbairn relates the problem of allegorical typology[12], "Like the Fathers, they [Glass, Cocceius, Witsius, and Vitringa] did not sufficiently distinguish between allegorical and typical interpretations, but regarded the one as only a particular form of the other, and both as equally warranted by the New Testament Scripture."[13]

Marsh writes, "that kind of allegorical interpretation . . . that may be properly called typical interpretation; for it is an application of types to their antitypes."[14] (To be clear with the terms, 'type' refers to "the persons, things, or events which forecast the age to come"[15] while 'antitype' refers to the later reality.) Marsh continues,

> Volumes have been filled with types and antitypes, which exist only in the fancy of the writers[16]. . . . If the inference be drawn without a proof of previous design and pre-ordained connection, we may still multiply our types and antitypes without end. Even the self-same type may be provided with various antitypes, according to the different views of the interpreters.[17]

To this Marsh provides the example of Cardinal Bellarmine who argued that

---

[12] The term 'allegorical typology' is a creation of this author to distinguish the typology that Marsh was responding to and the typology that Fairbairn and Ramm articulate and promote.

[13] Patrick Fairbairn, *Typology of Scripture, b1*, 11. On page 14, Fairbairn notes that it was the Marshian system that supplanted the Cocceian school of typology.

[14] Herbert Marsh, *Lectures on the Criticism and Interpretation and Interpretation of the Bible*, Kindle location 4458.

[15] Bernard Ramm, *Protestant Biblical Interpretation*, 216.

[16] Herbert Marsh, *Lectures on the Criticism and Interpretation and Interpretation of the Bible*, Kindle location 4492.

[17] ibid, Kindle location 4502.

the Protestant Reformation was typified in the secession of Israel under Jeroboam from Judah, which the Lutherans countered by arguing that Jeroboam's secession was typical of the Church of Rome abandoning primitive Christianity.[18]

Against this prolific use of allegorical typology, Marsh established a standard to curb its use:

> By what means shall we determine, in any given instance, that what is alleged as a type was really designed for a type? Its only possible source of interpretation is Scripture itself[19]. . ... Whatever persons, or things therefore, recorded in the Old Testament, were expressly declared by Christ, or his Apostles, to have been designed as pre-figurations of persons or things relating to the New Testament, such persons or things, so recorded in the former are types of the persons or things, with which they are compared in the latter.[20]

Answering Marsh

Certainly, the allegorical typology that Marsh encountered and was familiar with was of a species that is foreign to proper theology with its acrobatic use of the identification of type and antitype, and a prohibition against allegorical typology is warranted. Fairbairn agrees by writing,

> The Cocceian mode of handling the typical matter of ancient Scripture had no essential principles or fixed rules by which to guide its interpretation [and so] left room on every hand for arbitrariness and caprice to enter.[21]

Fairbairn then counters, "What solid ground or necessary reason is there for the principle that nothing less than inspired authority is sufficient to determine the reality and import of anything that is typical?"[22] He continues,

---

[18] ibid.

[19] ibid, Kindle location 4471.

[20] ibid, Kindle location 4481.

[21] Patrick Fairbairn, *Typology of Scripture,* b1, 13.
[22] ibid., 21.

> ... [Marshian typology] lies open to one objection. While the field was greatly circumscribed nothing was done in the way of investigating it internally, or of unfolding the grounds of connection between type and antitype. . . . With the very prescription of these limits, it wrongfully withholds from us the key of knowledge, and shuts us up to errors scarcely less to be deprecated than those it seeks to correct. For it destroys to a large extent the bond of connection between the Old and New Testament Scriptures.[23]

Additionally, Ramm points out,

> Marsh finds that in typology the facts and circumstances of one instance are *representative* of other facts and circumstances; whereas in allegorical interpretation they are emblematic. . . .. But if typological interpretation rises *naturally out of the text* then it is not an interpretation of *something else* and is therefore a method of interpretation within its own rights. Or, as Fairbairn puts it, the typical meaning "is not properly a different or higher sense [as allegorical interpretation demands], but a different or higher application *of the same sense*" . . . .. While some exegesis of the Old Testament in the name of typology is forced, to be sure, such excesses—past and present—do not destroy the Christian contention that the typological method of interpretation is valid.[24]

With typology, as with any skill, as one's understanding and discernment matures, the tools, techniques, and complexity of work likewise improves. Yet the research of typology was annexed from theological study by Bishop Marsh's standard. Fairbairn argues

> ... these typical characters and transactions should have the effect of prompting further inquiry rather than repressing it; since instead of themselves comprehending and bounding the whole field of Scriptural Typology they only exhibit practically the principles on which others of a like description are to be discovered and explained. [25]

---

[23] ibid., 20.

[24] Ramm, *Protestant Biblical Interpretation*, 225, 224, brackets are Ramm's insertion, quoting Patrick Fairbairn, *Typology of Scripture: Two Volumes in One* (Grand Rapids: Kregel Publications, 1989), b1, 3, 215, 259.

[25] Patrick Fairbairn, *Typology of Scripture*, b1, 22-23.

Among these materials Fairbairn includes Luke 24:27, "Then beginning with Moses and all the Prophets, [Jesus] interpreted for them the things concerning Himself in *all* the Scriptures"[26].

With their criticism of Marsh's strict standard and examination of the scriptural use of typology, Ramm and Fairbairn establish their own criteria for judging the veracity of a typological interpretation by examining and articulating the principles which the New Testament authors employed in their use of typology. Because of their reliance on Scripture for their standard it seems appropriate to follow Fairbairn's example above and refer to this as Scriptural Typology. By doing so, as Ramm implied above, they seek to establish typological interpretation as a school of interpretation separate from the allegorical school that it had been held under.

Scriptural Typology

Ramm's and Fairbairn's sets of criteria can be combined to form a standard by which to evaluate typological arguments and guard against the misuse of typology that Marsh was so familiar with (though this standard will stand primarily on Fairbairn since his book is focused on typology and Ramm's chapter tends to build on Fairbairn and a few others).

Fairbairn writes,

> Typological interpretation is the interpretation of the Old Testament based on the fundamental theological unity of the two testaments whereby something in the Old shadows, prefigures, adumbrates something in the New[27] . . . .. The general descriptions of the symbolical institutions of the Old Testament are of two classes; in the one they are declared to have been *shadows* of the better things of the Gospel . . . . In the second the religious institutions contained the *rudiments* or elementary principles of the world's religious truth and life.[28]

To this definition we can add Ramm,

---

[26] ibid., 216-217.

[27] ibid., 223.

[28] ibid., 55, 57.

> An *innate* type is a type specifically declared to be such by the New Testament. An *inferred* type is one that, not specifically designated in the New Testament is justified for its existence by the nature of the New Testament materials on typology . . . . An expanded typological interpretation was characteristic of the interpretations of the Old Testament by our Lord, by his apostles, and by the early church although in the latter it suffered from malpractice."[29]

To this the question must be asked regarding what Ramm and Fairbairn see as the nature of the New Testament materials.

The Nature of Types

Ramm appeals that

> the fact of prophecy establishes the principle that the New is latent in the Old, and the Old is patent in the New. The form of prophecy may be either verbally predictive or typically predictive . . . . Thus, a type is a species of prophecy. . . .[30]

Just as Jesus used earthly analogies to speak of heavenly things (John 3:12), the Old Testament uses types to foreshadow the things that would come to fulfillment through Jesus. This parallel between parable and type is inferred from Fairbairn's statement, "Viewing the institutions of the dispensation brought in by Moses as typical, we look at them in what may be called their *secondary aspect*; we consider them as *prophetic symbols of the better things to come in the Gospel*"[31]. He continues,

> The primary and essential elements of truth which are embodied in the facts of the Gospel can not be of recent origin. . . . Their existence must have formed the groundwork, and their varied manifestation the progress, of any preparatory dispensations . . . to the coming realities of the Gospel. Their more immediate intention and use must have consisted in the exhibition they gave of the vital and fundamental truths common alike to all dispensations. . . . Presenting the difficult to understand spiritual reality in a way that could more easily and distinctly be apprehended by the human mind.[32]

---

[29] Bernard Ramm, *Protestant Biblical Interpretation*, 220, 217, 259.

[30] ibid., 216.

[31] Patrick Fairbairn, *Typology of Scripture*, b1, 52.

This groundwork is to be "a partial exhibition of a *truth* or an embodiment of it in things more easily grasped by the understanding, but imperfectly satisfying the mind . . . that the mind thus familiarized may both have the desire created and the capacity formed for beholding its development in things of a far higher and nobler kind."[33]

To draw a parallel, one starts out learning arithmetic and works their way to higher and more complicated math, building upon the foundations that have been laid by the earlier, more tangible disciplines. So type joins with type until the picture comes into focus and one sees their principles and parts fulfilled in the Gospel of Jesus Christ.

Vocabulary

In their examination of Scriptural Typology, Fairbairn and Ramm take note of the "New Testament words referring to the nature of the Old Testament to establish the typical character of the Old Testament."[34] These are:
1. *Typos* and *typikos* (from the verb, *typto*, "to strike") meant the mark of a blow, the figure formed by a blow, an impression, a form, a letter, a doctrine, an example, a pattern, a type.
2. *Skia* (from *skene*, a tent) means a shade, a sketch, an outline, an adumbration.
3. The word type (τύπος) occurring once, at least, in the natural sense of *mark* or *impress* made by a hard substance on one of softer material (John 20:25), it commonly bears the general import of *model, pattern,* or *exemplar*.[35]

Ramm writes that types used in the New Testament fit into one of six categories, *1) Persons* (Elijah as the prefigurement of John the Baptist) 2) *Institutions* (Passover) 3) *Offices* (Priest) 4) *Events* (Wilderness wanderings) 5)

---

[32] ibid., 50-51.

[33] ibid., 52.

[34] ibid., 217-218.
[35] Bullets 1 and 2, Bernard Ramm, *Protestant Biblical Interpretation*, 217; Bullet 3, Patrick Fairbairn, *Typology of Scripture*, b1, 42.

Actions (lifting the bronze serpent) 6) *Things* (the Tabernacle).³⁶

Ramm adds, "These New Testament words referring to the nature of the Old Testament establish the typical character of the Old Testament. In addition to this is the weight of the entire book of Hebrews, for it is almost completely devoted to a study of the typical character of the Old Testament."³⁷

Setting the Boundaries

With the New Testament scope of the definition of type in hand it becomes necessary to examine the boundaries that the principles, observed by Fairbairn and Ramm, employed in the New Testament. Fairbairn writes,

> The symbolical institutions of the Old Covenant are not simply or directly representations of the Gospel, but expressive of certain great and fundamental truths, which could even then be distinctly understood and embraced. This might be called their more *immediate and ostensible* design. Their *further and prospective* reference to the higher objects of the Gospel were of a more indirect and [arcane] nature but stood in the same essential truths being exhibited by means of present and visible, but inferior and comparatively inadequate objects. So that, in tracing out the connection from the one to the other, we must always begin with inquiring, What, *per se*, was the native import of each symbol; what truths did it symbolize? and from this proceed to unfold how it was fitted to serve as a guide and a stepping-stone to the glorious events and issues of Messiah's kingdom. This—which it was the practice of the elder typological writers in great measure to overlook—is really the foundation of the whole matter.³⁸

It is a necessary inclusion to emphasize Fairbairn's description of types being "inferior and comparatively inadequate objects" and add the admonishment of Ramm, "*Dissimilarity* is to be expected. There is no one-to-one correspondence between type and antitype"³⁹.

---

³⁶ Bernard Ramm, *Protestant Biblical Interpretation*, 231-232.

³⁷ ibid., 217-218.

³⁸ Patrick Fairbairn, *Typology of Scripture*, b1, 53. The odd formatting of the fourth sentence is how Fairbairn wrote it.

As an example, Fairbairn examines John 3:14-15, where Jesus likens Himself to the bronze serpent by which the people of Israel were delivered from the plague of serpents in Numbers 21:4-9. To summarize Fairbairn,

> In both a wounded and dying condition, there a dying body, here a perishing soul; there the outward eye perceiving the object ordained for healing, here the spiritual eye looking in faith to the exalted Redeemer; in both the same mode of dealing, but there a temporal application, and here the unseen, spiritual, and eternal.[40]

To be sure the bronze serpent was flawed and was later destroyed because the people had begun worshiping it, rather than the One who established it (2 Kings 18:3-4). However, an examination of the events surrounding the bronze serpent reveals that the plague of venomous snakes was the Lord's judgment for Israel's rebellion against Him (vv. 5-6), an act of repentance on the part of the people preceded the appointing of the serpent (v. 7), and the raising of the serpent did not do away with the snakes altogether, but provided a way for the people to be saved from the venom's effects.

Fairbairn closes his comments on the bronze serpent by writing, "itself so extraordinary and peculiar, so unlike God's usual methods of dealing in providence it seems to be without any adequate reason until it is viewed as a dispensation specially designed to prepare the way for the higher and better things of the Gospel."[41]

Additionally, Neil Anderson, a noted deliverance minister, professor, and pastor expounds on Zechariah 3:1-4:

> Look at the cast of characters in this scene which resembles a heavenly courtroom. The judge is God the Father. The prosecuting attorney is Satan. The defense attorney is Jesus. And the accused defendant is Joshua the high priest, who represents all of God's people, including you and me . . . .. Satan the accuser says, "Look at him, God. He's filthy. He deserves to be struck dead." But God rebukes the accuser and puts him in his place . . . . Satan can't make his

---

[39] Bernard Ramm, *Protestant Biblical Interpretation*, 229.

[40] Patrick Fairbairn, Typology of Scripture, b1, 65-66.

[41] ibid, 66.

charges stick because Jesus Christ has justified us and lives to intercede for us (Rom. 8:33-34). God has not only declared us righteous, but He has removed our filthy garments of unrighteousness. Notice that the change of wardrobe is something that God does, not we ourselves. In ourselves we don't have any garments of righteousness to put on that will satisfy God.[42]

Nowhere in the New Testament is this scene referenced, let alone established as a type of the salvation worked out by Jesus. Therefore, an adherent of Marshian typology will not allow this interpretation because it is not explicitly used in the New Testament. Yet, what believer can help but look at it and see a prefiguring of the Gospel of Peace? In this way, those who hold to Marsh's standards contradict themselves and align with Fairbairn and Ramm's standards of Scriptural Typology.

Typology in Brief

In summary of the principles expounded upon above from Fairbairn and Ramm:

> Because the Old and New Testaments are linked[43] and the author of them prefigured the spiritual truths of the New in the Old,[44] there are people, institutions, offices, events, actions, and things which represent,[45] in limited and imperfect ways, truths of either spiritual or physical reality of the Gospel[46] in forms that are easier to grasp which help prepare the reader's mind for the difficult to understand fulfillment of the types.[47] These types must not be forced and must be of significant examples which were intended by God to fulfill this role through either inferred or innate means.[48] Because of their

---

[42] Neil Anderson, *The Bondage Breaker* (Eugene: Harvest House Publishers, 1990), 143-144.

[43] Patrick Fairbairn, *Typology of Scripture*, b1, 223.

[44] Bernard Ramm, Protestant Biblical Interpretation, 216.

[45] ibid., 231-232.
[46] Patrick Fairbairn, *Typology of Scripture*, b1, 53.

[47] ibid., b1, 52.

nature as inferior and comparatively inadequate objects of representation[49] of spiritual truth or principle of the Gospel, differences are to be expected.[50]

---

[48] Bernard Ramm, *Protestant Biblical Interpretation*, 220.

[49] Patrick Fairbairn, *Typology of Scripture*, b1, 53.

[50] Bernard Ramm, *Protestant Biblical Interpretation*, 229.

Shintō: the Gospel's Gate

CHAPTER 19: HEBREWS

Having examined the festival of Yom Kippur and the rules of typology, the question to answer is whether Leviticus 16 passes the tests of typological interpretation. The first test is if scripture uses the passage as a typological prophecy. The second test deals with whether the passage naturally fulfills the imagery we are trying to apply. Normally only one test would need to be validated, but because of the structure of Yom Kippur, it must pass both.

The first section of Hebrews opens by introducing the author's purpose of comparing the former revelation, given by prophets, with the revelation given by Jesus' life and death, whom the author calls the exact imprint of YHWH, who, after making purification for sins, sat down at the right hand of the Majesty on High (Heb. 1:1-3). The theme of suffering is introduced in 2:9-11 and is then contrasted with the victory over death and Satan in 2:14-15.

Hebrews 3:1 begins the second section with the transition, "therefore". Hebrews then compares Jesus as being greater than the former things, beginning with Moses. Chapters 3-10:18 follows the pattern of the old revelation, the superiority of Jesus, His completed work, the necessity of testing, and then the next comparison.

In the third section, from 10:19 to the end, the author begins to encourage the Christians to remain faithful and endure suffering by reminding them of the heroes of the faith, whom the author calls prophets.

Throughout the cycles of chapters 3-10:18, there are nine references to Jesus as high priest (3:1; 4:14, 15; 5:5, 10; 6:20; 7:24, 28; 8:1), entering beyond the veil three times (6:19; 7:25; 8:2), and offering himself two times (7:27; 8:3). The author is building upon the theme each time, laying the foundation for an argument and a final comparison. Notice that the three functions of high priest, entering in, and offering are listed in 8:1-3.

The author of Hebrews contrasts the Levitical priesthood's regulations with the superiority of Jesus through verses such as these:

> 7:11 "Now if perfection had been attainable through the Levitical priesthood, what further need would there have been for another priest to arise after the order of Melchizedek?"
>
> 7:18-19 "For on the one hand, a former commandment is set aside because of its weakness and uselessness, but on the other hand, a better hope is introduced, through which we draw near to God."
>
> 9:9b-10 "According to this arrangement, gifts and sacrifices are offered that cannot perfect the conscience of the worshiper; but deal only with food and drink and various washings, regulations for the body imposed until the time of reformation."
>
> 10:3-4 "In these sacrifices there is a reminder of sins every year. For it is impossible for the blood of bulls and goats to take away sins." (ESV)

The fullness of Christ's superiority is finally revealed in 9:11-14 and 21-26 (verses 15-20 regard the initiation of the Mosaic Covenant contrasted with the New Covenant). To summarize, Christ is the high priest who entered into the most holy place of the heavenly places, not the shadow of the tabernacle, whose blood cleanses our consciences so we can serve the living God (:11-14).

The true tabernacle had to be cleansed with better sacrifices than the blood of animals, so Christ entered the heavenly places by his own blood, once and for all, to bring about the removal of sin by the sacrifice of himself (:23-26).

The application to the individual is made in Hebrews 10:19-22,

> [19] . . . since we have confidence to enter the holy places by the blood of Jesus, [20] by the new way that he opened for us through the curtain, that is, through his flesh . . . [22] let us draw near with a true heart in full assurance of faith, with our hearts sprinkled clean from an evil conscience and our bodies washed with pure water. (ESV)

The burning of the bull and slain goat is also accounted for in 13:11-12. The application being that just as Jesus suffered outside the gate of Jerusalem, His disciples must leave the traditions and regulations of the Levitical priesthood, bearing the shame that this loss of belonging brings with it (:13). Jesus' High Priesthood was established in Melchizedek, before the establishment of the Levitical priesthood. Likewise, His service as High Priest takes place outside of the regulations and required festivals of the Levitical priesthood.

When we compare the events in Hebrews 9:11-14, 21-26, 10:19-22, and 13:11-12 with Yom Kippur, they account for the slain goat in Leviticus 16. The offering of the bull for the high priest's sins is accounted for in Hebrews 7:27, which says that Jesus did not need to make a sacrifice for himself because he had no sin.

This accounts for Leviticus 16:11-19 and :27, but what of the portion dealing with the live goat, which is "for Azazel"?

Azazel

It was stated earlier that the two goats were presented as a sin sacrifice, the two forming one whole (:5). Hebrews makes it clear that the sacrificed goat represented Jesus, who entered the heavenly places by his own blood. Because the two goats are one half of the whole, somehow the live goat must also represent Jesus.

The difficulty here is the translation that the live goat is sent to Azazel, understood to be the leader of demons. As we already saw, this interpretation mainly comes from the book of 1 Enoch, which has parallels to Akkadian magical and incantation texts.[1] However, Azazel is also translated as scapegoat, and in order to accommodate this, the particle ל *le* had to be rendered as "like" either by the KJV translators or William Tyndale.

If we then read Leviticus 16:10b and :25 as "like Azazel" the goat is placed solidly into typological language. The difference between לעזאזל *leAzazel* in :8 and :10a is that in these two verses the referent is to the lot, instead of the goat. Then we have "the lot for Azazel" twice (:8 and :10a) and the "goat like Azazel" and "the live goat sent into the wilderness like Azazel" (:10b and :25).

Is this a natural application? Each action done to the live goat has a corollary to the actions taken against Jesus. The high priest Caiaphas said it was better for one man to die than for the entire nation to perish. John then comments that Caiaphas did not realize he was prophesying by the Holy

---

[1] Aron Pinker, "Goat to Go to Azazel," *The Journal of Hebrew Scriptures* vol. 7, article 8, (2007): 18, doi:10.5508/jhs.2007.v7.a8, accessed 1-16-18.

Spirit (John 11:49-51). This parallels the high priest anointing the head of the live goat with the blood of the bull and the slain goat.

Whether the man at the ready represents Pontius Pilate specifically or the gentiles in general is hard to determine and is probably unimportant. The crucial point is that one of these groups are being represented by this 'man at the ready' who lead the live goat into the wilderness, away from the tabernacle.

Once the live goat is led away, the High Priest returns to the tent of meeting and takes off the linen robes, folds them, and then dresses in his normal clothing to return to the congregation. After Jesus' death, he was wrapped in linen, probably white, and placed in Joseph's tomb (Luke 23:53, 24:12; John 19:40, 20:6-7). When the two disciples entered the empty tomb, they saw the linen burial clothes and the head covering folded and laid on the body-slab.

Considering this evidence, it seems that the live goat is indeed representing Jesus. Consider the typological application of Yom Kippur and the slain goat by the author of Hebrews, and the similarity of the three actions upon the live goat and Jesus. Since לעזאזל *leAzazel* should be understood as "like Azazel" the antitype for Azazel is Jesus himself. Azazel is then not the name or title of the live goat, nor the name of a demon, but is a typological reference to Jesus. This author's theory of עָזַב *azav* plus אֶל *el* as "the God who removes our impurity" is reasonably supported by scripture itself.

Sequence

There is the question of why Yom Kippur demonstrates the spiritual before the physical reality of Jesus' crucifixion. There are three explanations that help answer this question. First, according to the rules of typology there are differences between type and anti-type. Second, it is impossible to imagine how the live goat could be seen carrying away the impurities of the tabernacle if it was sent out first. Third when prophecy addresses both physical and spiritual realities, it is normal to see the spiritual reality addressed before the physical reality. Table 19.1 aligns the events of Lev. 16 with the NT anti-type.

Quick Quote	Type	Anti-Type	Quick Quote
Preparation			
Cleansing Tabernacle	Lev 16	Heb 8:5 Heb 9:23	Shadow and Copy
Blood of bull and goat	:3	Heb 9:23b	Better sacrifice
Linen Clothes	:4	John 20:40	Wrapped in linen
Wash his body	:5	John 20:39	Perfume Anointed
Bull for himself	:6	Heb 7:27	Did not need
Lots for two goats	:7-8		Two goats, one sacrifice
Lots: One for YHWH, one for Azazel	:8	John 1:29	Behold the Lamb of God
Goat sacrificed	:9	John 20:17-30	Crucifixion
Goat like Azazel	:10b	Heb 9:26 Heb 9:28	Removal of sins by himself Bears iniquity
Completion			
Sacrifice bull	:11	Heb 7:27	No need
Enter the Holy of Holies	:12	Heb 9:6-9, 10:20	Way was not made clear Through His flesh
Blood in Holy of Holies	:14, 15	Heb 9:12	His own blood
Cleanse the Tabernacle	:16-19	Heb 9:23	Heavenly Places
Confession	:20-21	John 11:49-51	better one man perish.
Man at the Ready	:21	John 18:28-19:18	Given to Romans
To Barren Place	:22	John 19:17	Brought to Golgotha
Bear the iniquity	:22	Heb 9:28	bore the sins of many
Send goat away	:22	John 19:17	to Golgotha
Fold Clothes	:23	John 20:5-6	Folded linen

Table 19.1 Type and Antitype

Like YHWH?

Another question is, "If the second goat is *like* Azazel, should we not say that the first goat is like YHWH?" The answer is that the original Hebrew does not use the grouping of ליהוה *leYHWH* for the first goat. The goat that is slain is simply referred to by the lot through which it was designated for

YHWH. This means that the second goat, the live goat, alone carries the explicit typological name.

What is the difference?

The live goat is specifically enacting the process by which Jesus would be designated for arrest by the High Priest, then tried and brought out to Golgotha by the Gentiles. The live goat is performing an action by carrying the עָוֹן *ayon*, פֶּשַׁע *peshah*, חָטָא *chata*, and טמא *tumah* of Israel.

The slain goat is simply slain, it performs no action. Its blood is acted upon to cleanse the tabernacle and the people of Israel, so in this, Hebrews also parallels the slain goat to Jesus, as a representative of Jesus' actions in the Heavenly places.

Forgiveness or Cleansing?

With the flexibility of typological prophecy, Jesus is being represented by the high priest, the live goat, and the slain goat. One of the immediate consequences of this interpretation is that we must question whether we are required to think of the Gospel as forgiveness of sins. Yom Kippur and Hebrews clearly use the idea of being cleansed from sin, so passages translated as being forgiven of sin should be reconsidered in light of this Biblical portrayal of atonement.

For instance, the Greek word ἄφεσις *aphesis* is translated as forgiveness in the majority of English translations. Yet the KJV translated ἄφεσις *aphesis* as remission, which has the idea of carrying away or removing, similar in use as speaking of the remission of cancer. The later Roman emphasis on guilt and innocence is therefore superimposed upon the Hebrew mindset of cleansing, resulting in a form of theological syncretism.[2]

Pronunciation

When I first shared this theory of לעזאזל *leAzazel* as an elision עזב *azav* plus אל *el* with Dr. Benjamin Noonan at Columbia International University, one of his initial insights was to ask how a 'compensatory shortening' of the

---

[2] Jackson Wu, "The Yin-Yang of Contextualization," Patheos, accessed 8-24-16, posted 8-23-16, http://www.patheos.com/blogs/jacksonwu/2016/08/23/the-yin-yang-of-contextualization/

consonant could be supported by other Hebrew extant texts. He also asked how the ב *bet* could shorten to ז *zayin*.

After consideration, I have a few answers to his challenge. First, extant writing is not the only source that can or should be considered, so I will stand with the typological evidence instead. As for the oddity of the ב *bet* shortening to ז *zayin*, I would argue that Hebrew is not tied to English phonetic relationships.

For instance, if one asked an English speaker how the 'b' sound is related to the 'h' sound, they would respond that there is no relationship. Yet a Japanese speaker would immediately say that the 'b' is a voiced 'h' as indicated with the dakuten next to the character は *ha* → ば *ba*.

So with the consideration of the consonant change in Azazel, the 'b' sound is produced with both lips popping voiced, while the 'v' sound is produced with the top teeth on the bottom lip voiced, and the 'z' sound is produced with the upper and bottom teeth voiced. The result is that the 'b' takes the longest to produce, while the 'z' is shortest. In my theory then, the v shortens to z to indicate the switched positions of the א *aleph* and the ב *bet*. The logic being that the sounds are produced with vocalization at the front of the mouth.

Another consideration is that, as a proper name, Azazel may violate the normal pattern of Hebrew syllable rules and introduce an alteration for the sake of disambiguation. As Proverbs 25:2 says, "It is the glory of God to conceal things, but the glory of kings to search things out." (ESV)

Early Theological Thought

Another consideration to address is the early thoughts of the church scholars, such as the so-called Church Fathers and Ante-Nicene Church Fathers. With time constraints and the intended length of this book, an exhaustive survey of these writers is prohibited. However, we can introduce two positive examples of such writing. The first comes from Cyril of Alexandria and the other from Tertullian.

Cyril of Alexandria wrote

> It was fitting, therefore, that the law given through Moses, since its intention was to delineate the mystery of Christ, should not present him by one of the goats or one of the birds, dying and living at the same time, lest the

deed might seem to be somehow a wonder-working show, but it regards him in one of them as suffering his immolation, and presents him in the other as living and having been set free.[3]

Accordingly, the law was a picture and, in the law, the types of things were fertile with the truth, with the result that even if the precept introduced two goats to illustrate the mystery of Christ and even if there were two birds, he in both was one, both in suffering and beyond suffering, and in death and over death and ascending in the heavens...[4]

Now to look at Tertullian.

If I may offer, moreover, an interpretation of the two goats which were presented on "the great day of atonement," do they not also figure the two natures of Christ? . . . One of these goats was bound with scarlet, and driven by the people out of the camp into the wilderness, amid cursing, and spitting, and pulling, and piercing, being thus marked with all the signs of the Lord's own passion; while the other, by being offered up for sins, and given to the priests of the temple for meat, afforded proofs of His second appearance.[5]

Cyril sees in the first goat Jesus in heaven, though how exactly is not made clear – is this speaking of Jesus' resurrection, or of his ascension, or of Hebrews' typological portrayal? – and he delineates the second goat as representing Christ's suffering. Tertullian is briefer with his application of the two goats, seeing in the live goat Jesus' suffering and in the slain goat evidence of Christ's second appearance.

The common weakness between Cyril and Tertullian is that neither make a direct comment on the name of Azazel, whether positive or negative. Their focus instead was on the two goats by themselves. Both authors saw the two goats as one representation of Jesus, though their application of the live goat differed from each other. Neither interpretation naturally apply themselves to a basic reading of Leviticus 16, failing the test of typological interpretation.

---

[3] Cyril of Alexandria, *Letters of St. Cyril of Alexandria, volume 1*, trans. John I. McEnerney (Washington: Catholic University of America Press, 1987), 180.

[4] ibid., 181.

[5] Alexander Roberts and James Donaldson, editors, *Ante-Nicene Fathers, Volume 3, Latin Christianity: Its Founder, Tertullian. I. Apologetic; II. Anti-Marcion; III, Ethical* (Hendrickson Publishers, 2004), book III, chapter 7, 327.

Shintō: the Gospel's Gate

It is probably because of this last factor that the interpretation of Azazel as pointing toward Christ has not been more prevalent in the church.

Lamb or Goat?

Our final obstacle for applying the typological interpretation of Azazel is how to reconcile a goat representing Jesus when John the Baptist says, "Behold the Lamb of God who takes away the sin of the world!" (ESV) Normally, when people read this verse they have been conditioned by endless repetition to think of the Passover Lamb. However, there are two issues with this.

First, the Passover Lamb is not portrayed as taking away sin, its function is to rescue the Hebrews from the Angel of Death, therefore this typological symbolism fails the typological test. Secondly, a careful reading of Exodus reveals that the Passover Lamb could be taken from the sheep or the goats.

What animal did the Hebrews picture when they used the word for lamb? There are three words that are key to research to properly understand this aspect of the Hebrew mindset. It is an incredibly insignificant area of study; however, the question becomes pertinent because of the seriousness and focus of the present consideration of Azazel.

The Hebrew word for lamb is שֶׂה *seh* and occurs 46 times in 39 verses of the Bible. The concordance provides the definition of lamb and sheep for שֶׂה *seh*, but *why* would the Hebrews would use a word interchangeably. There are clear verses that place שֶׂה *seh* as lamb, not sheep.

> Exodus 12:5 "your שֶׂה lamb shall be unblemished . . . taken from the כֶּשֶׂב *kishev* sheep or the עֵז *ez* goats.
> Leviticus 5:6-7 … a female from the flock, a כֶּשֶׂב *kishev* sheep or a עֵז *ez* goat… but if he cannot afford a שֶׂה *seh* lamb…
> Deuteronomy 14:4 you may eat: the ox, the שֶׂה sheep the שֶׂה goat. Literally, Deuteronomy 14:4 reads שֵׂה כְשָׂבִים וְשֵׂה עִזִּים *seh k'savim v'seh 'izim* "the lamb from the sheep and the lamb from the goats".

In total, שֶׂה *seh* is rendered as sheep, flock, or another word inappropriately 26 times – over half of the occurrences of שֶׂה *seh* in the Hebrew Bible.

The Hebrew word for sheep has two forms, כֶּבֶשׂ *keves* (152x) and כֶּשֶׂב

kesev (13x) at least one source suggests that this was because of a scribal error reversing the *bet* with the *sin*. There seems to be a linguistic preference of the translators to render these as lamb when speaking of sacrifices, and to gloss the phrase "a one-year-old sheep" as "a lamb".

Such glosses occur 106 of 165 times in the Hebrew bible. Listing the positive or the negative examples would be tedious. It should be noted that the percentage of sheep being mis-labeled as lamb is skewed because of the Hebrew convention of repeating כֶּבֶשׂ *keves* to indicate a male sheep. Such doubling happens 36 times, making 129 individual uses of כֶּבֶשׂ *keves*, indicating an 82% ratio of miss-translation of sheep as lamb.

The relationship between sheep, goat, and lamb can be visually represented by figure 19.1.

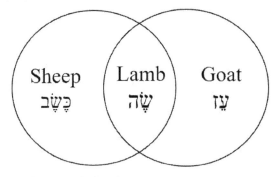

Figure 19.1 Lamb

Between the inappropriate glosses of כֶּבֶשׂ *keves* and שֶׂה *seh* 132 of 155 or 85% are glossed to fit the English convention of a lamb being a sheep. Regarding the Lamb of God, it is only necessary to consider the verses explicitly listed for examples in שֶׂה *seh* to establish that lamb in the Hebrew mind can be either a goat or a sheep. Therefore, there is no problem with viewing the live goat of Leviticus 16 as the Lamb of God which John was referencing.

CHAPTER 20: ANALOGY AND APPLICATION

The danger in developing a redemptive analogy as an outsider, is that there could still be a cultural superiority that subtly asserts that Western forms of Christianity are superior to Japanese forms. We can put the Gospel into Japanese terms, but are we willing to let the Japanese express Christianity in Japanese cultural forms?

As pointed out earlier, it was not until the Western missionaries were kicked out of China that the Chinese Church became indigenous and truly multiplied. What does a truly Japanese Church look like? How do they worship? How do they celebrate the Feasts of Israel and Communion? Not just a Japanese Church with Western forms, but a truly Japanese church expressing Christian truth and identity in Japanese cultural forms.

I am certain that this is one of the sources of resistance to the Gospel in Japan. Western missionaries and theologians, since the time of the Holy Roman Empire, have come into a culture and sought to impose their culture upon the host culture. Effectively, we miss the fact that our own culture needs to be redeemed. Our approach should not be to compare the host culture to our culture, but to see where both cultures deviate from the ideal culture that Israel was supposed to walk in with 上帝 Jōtei. Figure 20.1 shows this flaw.

In column A, Western culture simply ignores biblical culture and uses its own thinking to bring theological thought into a new culture. The insistence of sin as 'missing the mark' instead of seeking to understand the Hebrew mindset is one such example.

In column B, Western culture interacts with biblical culture by imposing its own structures and culture upon biblical culture and only bringing back those things which have been forced to fit Western culture. This is then used to bring Western theological thought into the host culture.

Shintō: the Gospel's Gate

In column C, Western thought engages with and conforms to biblical culture and thought, which is then brought to the host culture to the best of the practitioner's ability.

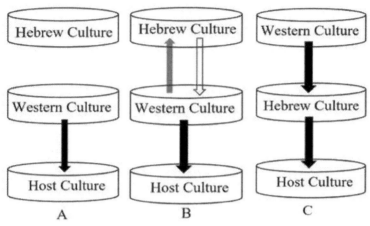

Figure 20.1 Culture Drum

Hopefully, I have been mindful enough to engage with Hebrew culture and allow it to change my theological assumptions. Then, hopefully, I have been mindful enough to look at Japanese culture without pre-judging it. These two steps should allow us to see where there are practices and ideas in Japan that parallel Hebrew culture and practices. I believe that through this comparison, Shintō is the Gospel's Gate by which salvation can be communicated to the Japanese.

Shared Focus

At this point, we have examined Israel and Shintō practices for dealing with the impurity (טֻמְאָה *tumah* and 穢れ *kegare*) which result from our sin (עָוֹן *ayon*, פֶּשַׁע *peshah*, and חָטָא *chata* and 罪 *tsumi*) and prevent us from having fellowship with YHWH or the kami, respectively. We have also examined how the book of Hebrews uses Yom Kippur to explain the Gospel to the Hebrews, comparing Jesus to the High Priest and the two goats. What remains is for us to ask how we can use the similarity of お祓い Oharai and Yom Kippur to explain the Gospel to the Japanese.

The problem with using the High Priest is that in Japan, the High Priest of

144

Shintō: the Gospel's Gate

Shintō is the Emperor of Japan. How could we use the analogy of the High Priest and guard against confusion of terms? This difficulty makes the analogy inappropriate.

Our second option is to use the 人形 *hitogata*, also called the 撫物 *nademono*, 形代 *katashiro*, 贖物 *agamono*, and rendered into English as scapegoat. The focal point of Yom Kippur, the climax of the action, is the live goat, who is like Azazel. Thus, the natural focus of Leviticus 16 and the similarity with お祓い Oharai is the scapegoat.

I would suggest that a first step needs to be an honest appreciation of Shintō and establishing an understanding of the purpose of お祓い Oharai. As an outsider, this can be done by asking questions and reading a book or visiting the Shintō Shrine together to observe お祓い Oharai and ask questions of the 巫女 Miko (Shrine Maiden) and 神主 Kannushi (Shintō Priest). As a Japanese Christian, it should be somewhat easier to engage with the seeker in a discussion about Shintō and お祓い Oharai – but this is a large assumption on my part. It will vary from person to person since Japanese people do not want to appear uninformed about their own culture.

By asking questions about お祓い Oharai, we may find that our seeker friend is already knowledgeable and perhaps even stopped going to the 神社 Jinja because they found the cleansing of お祓い Oharai did not have lasting results. This is a person who is truly seeking and spiritually sensitive. Also, if our Japanese friend was not aware of the ritual, we have introduced it to them without any direct exposure of their ignorance.

It is best if the seeker articulates the purpose of the 贖物 *agamono* so that we can ask, "What does this mean to you?" allowing them to personalize this new or re-found knowledge.

Once cleansing or sin removal is established, we can take them to Leviticus 16 and do an evangelistic bible study examining Yom Kippur, and the expounding of the Prophets about 上帝 Jōtei carrying away our sin. Again, I will stress, it needs to be the seeker who articulates the meaning of the Crucifixion and the connection to お祓い Oharai. There is just something about a person seeing and saying it for themselves which makes its way deeper into the heart and has a greater impact on the individual.

The exact wording and explanation will have to be refined and adjusted by Japanese Christians and those foreign ministry workers who have a better

神男 Shinotoko

Following our establishment of the お祓い Oharai analogy, we can also then use the example of the Konomiya Jinja Hadaka Matsuri as a form of the Crucifixion of Jesus.

Let us review: a man is selected to bear the impurities and sin of the community as the 神男 *Shinotoko*; he is secluded in the 神社 Jinja for three days; on the third day, he is removed from the Shrine and the assembled men strike him to transfer their impurities and sin; then the 神男 Shinotoko carries rice representing the 罪 *tsumi* and 穢れ *kegare* he accumulated and buries it, thereby purifying all the participants. Until the Tokugawa era this ritual involved real human sacrifice, as demonstrated by Kato Genchi.

The parallel to the crucifixion is striking. The chronology of the Hadaka Matsuri has the three days in the grave, the crucifixion, and then the resurrection. All the elements of the crucifixion are present, just as the spiritual and physical events are reversed in Yom Kippur.

The relevant passages of a Gospel and the book of Hebrews should be studied after this, to help the seeker see the connection between the Scapegoat, the Crucifixion, and the Christian faith.

These two analogies and an understanding of the Gospel in terms of shame-honor and purity-impurity will help the Japanese understand the Christian faith and demonstrate that this is not a foreign religion. The Gospel has been demonstrated to the Japanese through お祓い Oharai from the beginning of their history. And the crucifixion has been acted out through various 裸祭り Hadaka Matsuri for several hundred years. The Gospel of Jesus is the fulfillment of what Shintō has been searching for.

The summary of the Gospel for the Japanese would essentially be, "We have inherited 穢れ kegare from our ancestors and therefore have committed 罪 tsumi and created our own 穢れ kegare, which separates us from 上帝 Jōtei, who is 天之御中主の神 Amenominakanushi no Kami. To restore His honor, and rescue us from sin and death, 上帝 Jōtei sent Jesus to be the final 贖物 agamono and take away the 罪 tsumi and 穢れ kegare of those who trust in Him. Jesus is our 贖物 agamono, our ransom, who restores us to our created purpose of fellowship with 上帝 Jōtei."

This summary will need to be refined according to the Japanese seeker and the style of the Japanese Christian or foreign evangelist, whether they are a lay person or a professional minister. It is my hope that all Japanese Christians and Christians who are friends with Japanese seekers will be able to learn and use this redemptive analogy.

The harvest is too great to leave the task of evangelism and discipleship to the pastors and missionaries. As it is written, "And he gave the apostles, the prophets, the evangelists, the shepherds, and teachers to equip the saints for the work of ministry, for building up the body of Christ" (Eph. 4:11-12, ESV).

Visual Aid

An idea to help visualize and ritualize the scapegoat revolves around the celebration of Easter. At one of the churches I attended in the United States, on Easter morning people came with flowers and pinned them to a wooden cross that had been erected in the courtyard. Japanese Christians could visually and ritually represent the scapegoat by making a sculpture of the High Priest placing his hands on the head of either a goat, such as the serow, or a deer, such as found in Nara park.

Then as part of Easter celebrations, Christians could place objects like flowers or pieces of paper on the goat's head and back. Not as a way of being cleansed for the next year but as a reminder that Jesus, the true Azazel, has already carried away their sin and impurity. It is a way to remind people of the story of the Bible, of salvation, and the types and anti-types that 上帝 Jōtei imbedded into scripture.

Into the Sea

There is much more that can be said and developed about how Shintō parallels the Gospel in terms of お祓い Oharai. As a case in point, there is a parallel between the prayer, "The great gods of the purification-place will take out into the river and sea all sorts of offences . . . and blow them away and completely banish them and get rid of them into Hades"[1] and Micah 7:19, "And you will hurl all their sins into the depths of the sea." (ESV)

This verse deserves special consideration and a closer look. In full, Micah 7:19 reads, "He will again have compassion on us; he will trample our iniquities. And you will hurl all their sins into the depths of the sea."

This verse provides two places of apparent discord: the change in pronouns and how do trampled sins get hurled into the sea?

First, we can deal with the change in pronoun "us" and "their" by realizing that Micah is prophesying about a future action. 上帝 Jōtei is having mercy on us – Israel – but in a future time when none of the original audience is alive. The second pronoun change of he to you evokes an image of Micah speaking first to the Israelites and then addressing 上帝 Jōtei and describing the work to be accomplished, which is a device used by other prophets.

The third issue can be solved when we look at the original Hebrew. The word for trample is כָּבַשׁ *kâbash* which means to tread down, conquer, subjugate, bring into bondage.[2] Nehemiah 5:5 uses כָּבַשׁ *kâbash* to speak of Israel's children being brought into slavery.

Imagery of sin being trampled down and then thrown into the sea feels contradictory. How does the one lead to the other? But if we consider an alternative rendering of "gather" from the meaning "bring into bondage" the imagery then works better. Somehow the sin of Israel is gathered together and then thrown into the sea like some giant rock as "hurl" suggests.

Such imagery of Israel's sin being gathered together and sent away would also correlate to the Yom Kippur imagery of sin being placed upon the live goat, as if it was some package or burden.

To further the tension of compassion and trample, Barker notes that, "The Hebrew for "compassion" [רָחַם *racham*] suggests a tender, maternal love such as a mother would have for her child."[3] Such a word does not fit

---

[1] Karl Florenz and Ernest Mason Satow, *Ancient Japanese Rituals and the Revival of Pure Shintō*, 44-45.
See footnote 17 in the chapter, Shintō: Oharai.

[2] J. Strong, *A Concise Dictionary of the Words in the Greek Testament and The Hebrew Bible*, vol. 2(Bellingham, WA: Logos Bible Software, 2009), 54.

[3] K. L. Barker, *Micah, Nahum, Habakkuk, Zephaniah, Vol. 20* (Nashville: Broadman &

the mood of a violent action as trampling suggests.

Instead of the warrior king, we see the compassionate mother. She comes to her disobedient child who has fallen into the filth of the road and hurt him or herself and gathers her child into her arms. She gently washes her child while singing a comforting song, treats any wounds, and then dresses her precious child in fresh clothes. She then takes the filthy, smelly water and throws it into the river so that it is carried to the sea. Mother then returns to her child to play and teach gently, demonstrating her love. Wrath has no place in her heart, her desire is to show how precious her child is to her.

Micah 7:19 would thus read, "He will again have compassion on us; he will gather our iniquities together. You will hurl all their sins into the depths of the sea." Instead of bearing the sin and impurity to the desert, the offensive material is sent to the depths of the ocean where no person could access it.

Isaiah 66:13 also uses such maternal imagery. It reads, "As one whom his mother comforts, so I will comfort you, and you shall be comforted in Jerusalem." (ESV) Such maternal imagery is perfectly in line with Jesus' statement in Matthew 23:37 comparing himself to a hen who gathers her chicks under her wings.

This awareness of the maternal language of Micah 7:19 and Isaiah 66:13 helps us to address another barrier to the Japanese acceptance of the Gospel. The barrier of father imagery, which many who have suffered abandonment or abuse from their father or father figure struggle with. Shusaku Endo gives a window into the Japanese perspective.

> But the image of God that John [the Baptist] embraced was a father-image–the image of wrath, and judgement, and punishment. It was the image of a grim, censorious deity . . . like a despotic father, punishing without mercy the perfidy of all human beings.[4]

Having access to an explanation of salvation through the maternal vein of washing and comforting will certainly be able to aid the Japanese in explaining and understanding the Gospel. This time of researching and developing this redemptive analogy has had a profound impact on my own

---

Holman Publishers, 1999), 134–135.

[4] Shusaku Endo, *A Life of Jesus,* trans. Richard A. Schuchert (Ramsey: Paulist Press, 1973), 24.

understanding and appreciation of the Gospel.

Differences

While similarities of ideas in the scapegoat carrying away 罪 tsumi and 穢れ kegare do exist, there are also many ways in which Shintō is at odds with the imagery of the Bible. Panenpolypneumism against theism; worship of one Creator against the worship of many spirits; death and reintegration against death and everlasting reward or punishment; etc. How then can we engage with Shintō, the foundation of Japanese culture without compromising the Gospel?

I can see two ways to engage with Shintō without compromise. The first is to follow Paul's example in Acts 17:22-27

> [22] So Paul, standing in the midst of the Areopagus, said: "Men of Athens, I perceive that in every way you are very religious. [23] For as I passed along and observed the objects of your worship, I found also an altar with this inscription: 'To the unknown god.' What therefore you worship as unknown, this I proclaim to you. [24] The God who made the world and everything in it, being Lord of heaven and earth, does not live in temples made by man, [25] nor is he served by human hands, as though he needed anything, since he himself gives to all mankind life and breath and everything. [26] And he made from one man every nation of mankind to live on all the face of the earth, having determined allotted periods and the boundaries of their dwelling place, [27] that they should seek God, and perhaps feel their way toward him and find him." (ESV)

Paul notices the one good thing about the Greek's spiritual practices and praises them for their deep religious convictions. In this evangelistic speech, Paul makes no comment on the drinking of blood, worshiping idols, child and animal prostitutes, orgies, or death sports.

In the same way, we can speak and acknowledge the Japanese' deep spiritual sense and their model of the 神男 Shinotoko in the 人形 hitogata. Instead of "what you worship as unknown" we could replace with "I declare to you the true 神男 Shinotoko." It is in this way that we can turn the momentum of Shintō toward helping to proclaim the Gospel. Instead of being a barrier to the Gospel, Shintō is the Gospel's gate.

The second way to engage with Shintō without compromise follows

Shintō: the Gospel's Gate

Toyohiko Kagawa's admonition, "If Christians give evidence that they also have a high appreciation of Japan's past and its culture, it will help non-Christians to understand the true spirit of the Christian faith."[5] For this, the model comes from the author of Hebrews.

While the author pointed out the insufficiency of the Levitical priesthood, the author did so without a tone of contempt or superiority. In the same way we can speak of Shintō as having elements that are praiseworthy, while gently and respectfully (1 Peter 3:15) explaining how Jesus is superior to お祓い Oharai.

Perhaps one strategy is that we can address the shortcomings of the Levitical purification rites with its established parallels to Shintō. Thereby we avoid direct criticism of Japanese culture, while using the same exact words. An additional advantage of this is that the words of criticism are being spoken from nearly 2000 years ago and carry the very authority of the Holy Spirit (2 Tim 3:16).

---

[5] Toyohiko Kagawa, *Christ and Japan*, trans. William Axling (New York: Friendship Press, 1934), 88-89.

Shintō: the Gospel's Gate

CHAPTER 21: ANSWERING THE CHALLENGE

The drama of Scripture began with Satan's honor challenge in the Garden of Eden. Adam listened and ate from the forbidden fruit and was separated from the Creator because of his sin and impurity. Yet even as 上帝 Jōtei pronounced the curse upon the serpent, He also predicted how the serpent would be overcome by the seed of the woman. In time, this prediction was fulfilled through Jesus.

Every character has a motivation, and this is true for Jesus as well. Simply said, Jesus motivation was to restore the honor of 上帝 Jōtei and mend the relationship with humanity by removing sin and conquering death. In his identity as Azazel, Jesus removes sin from the hearts of those who trust in Him. Through his self-caused resurrection, Jesus conquered death.

Honor Triad

Jesus' identity was marked by trust in 上帝 Jōtei as the Father of Creation and from this Jesus received honor, authority, and security. This is nearly identical to the triad Adam originally walked in, with the key difference that Adam was innocent; that is, he had no knowledge of good and evil. When Adam was tested, he placed his trust in himself, manifesting as greed. In contrast, Jesus already understood good and evil, and when he was tested, he proved that his trust was in 上帝 Jōtei.

An expression of the honor which 上帝 Jōtei gave Jesus was the authority that he walked in. Instead of fearing spirits, disease, and nature, Jesus had authority over these forces. There was no competition or magic formulae through which Jesus did these things, it was how 上帝 Jōtei had originally designed mankind to rule over the natural world. Instead of fighting for control, Jesus had the security of knowing who He was and the purpose of

Shintō: the Gospel's Gate

his life. I consider this to be the stative expression (intrinsic identity) of who Jesus is.

Jesus was able to walk in his role as Azazel because of his trust in 上帝 Jōtei. This defined his identity, or motivation, in life. He lived to restore, or redeem, the honor of 上帝 Jōtei and the relationship between 上帝 Jōtei and humanity. Jesus did this through the role of a servant of 上帝 Jōtei and offered himself as a ransom to rescue humanity from the power of sin and death. This is summed up in Matthew 20:28 ". . . the Son of Man came not to be served but to serve and to give his life as a ransom for many."

I express the Honor Triad, with its stative and motivational sides, in figure 21.1. The stative side is trust, honor, authority, and security, while the motivation side is identity, redeem, rescue, and serve.

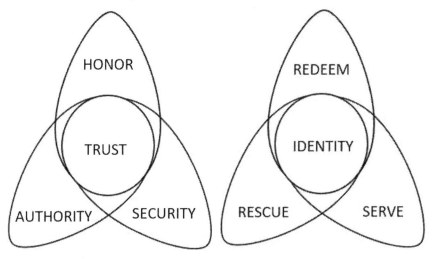

Figure 21.1 Honor Triad

This contrasts with the stative and motivation triads seen in a fallen humanity. With an identity marred by sin, the stative side (greed, shame, fear, and strife) is antagonistic to the motivational side (self, earned honor, power, and control). With a self that is not affected by sin, the stative and motivation sides are complimentary and reinforce each other.

On the Cross

In the propitiation model of salvation, Jesus endures 上帝 Jōtei's wrath for sin through the torture and crucifixion at the hands of the Romans. One theologian explained that "because Jesus is infinitely valuable, his suffering has infinite merit." This has been one of the major hurdles for proponents of the theory of expiation, that Jesus carried away sin. The answer lies, once again, in seeing the Scripture as a drama with three characters: 上帝 Jōtei, humanity, and Satan.

Before Jesus began to demonstrate his authority over demons, disease, and death, He endured forty days of fasting and temptation in the desert. At the end of forty days, Satan tempted Jesus to turn rocks into bread (Matt. 4:3, Luke 4:3), to throw himself from the top of the temple (Matt. 4:5, Luke 4:9), and to receive power through Satan himself (Matt. 4:8-9, Luke 4:5-7). After Jesus rebuked Satan, Luke 4:13 says that "[the devil] departed until an opportune time." (ESV) That more opportune time was the crucifixion.

We can draw a parallel between Jesus and Job. In Job 1, Satan asserted that Job only worshipped 上帝 Jōtei because of the things 上帝 Jōtei did for him, but if he suffered loss, Job would curse 上帝 Jōtei to his face (1:9-11). However, Job remained loyal to 上帝 Jōtei and stood against Satan's test. Then, in Job 2:4-5, Satan said that Job would turn away from 上帝 Jōtei if he faced physical suffering. Despite the losses and suffering that Job endured, he remained faithful to 上帝 Jōtei.

After these trials, 上帝 Jōtei blessed Job more than the blessings he had at the beginning of Satan's testing (42:10, 12). In the same way, Jesus passed the first test of physical loss through fasting and wilderness wandering. The second test came as Satan entered Judas, who betrayed Jesus to the rulers of Israel (Luke 22:3), the iniquity of the Sanhedrin, and the cruelty of the Romans.

Satan prefaced the first two temptations in the desert with "If you are the Son of God" (Mat. 4:3, :5), words that the Pharisees and others repeat as Jesus hangs on the cross. "If you are the Son of God, come down from the cross." (Matt. 27:40, Mark 15:29-31, Luke 23:35-38)

Once again, Satan was meeting with the Son of God at a tree tempting him to take control of his own life (Luke 3:38 calls Adam the son of God). If Jesus calls out for legions of angels to save him (Mat. 26:53) then 上帝 Jōtei withholds his best and Satan wins. If Jesus refuses to die and comes off the cross, the prophecies are left unfulfilled and Satan wins. If Jesus dies and does not rise again, Satan wins.

It is not 上帝 Jōtei's wrath, but Satan's wrath, that Jesus is enduring. Jesus rescued others who were being tormented by demons, now Satan has the opportunity to torture and kill the Son of God. For three years, Jesus has demonstrated his authority over the power of Satan, sin, and death. Through this one man, the honor of 上帝 Jōtei was partially restored. But then 上帝 Jōtei suffers a greater loss when Jesus dies on the cross, and Satan seems triumphant.

But the story does not end at the Cross, because Jesus rises from the dead early on the first day of the week (Matt. 28:1-6; Mark 16:2-7; Luke 24:1-7; John 20:1), fulfilling the prophecies, and proving his claim to be the Son of God.

It is through Jesus that 上帝 Jōtei answers Satan's honor challenge. Satan's original honor challenge was that 1) 上帝 Jōtei cannot be trusted, 2) He is holding back the very best from you, and 3) you will not die. Jesus proved 上帝 Jōtei is to be trusted because he kept his promise to destroy the serpent and restore humanity to relationship. Through Jesus, 上帝 Jōtei gave his very best, his one and only son (John 3:16). Jesus overcame death and those who trust in him shall not die (John 5:24, 26; 11:25).

This is the more complex honor challenge where 上帝 Jōtei's reputation before humanity is enhanced from what it was before Adam's rebellion. To be clear 上帝 Jōtei's honor is enhanced qualitatively, not quantitatively. Humanity experiences and appreciates 上帝 Jōtei's honor more because of what 上帝 Jōtei has done. 上帝 Jōtei does not change; our understanding of Him does.

The simplistic Gospel explanation of "Jesus loved us so much that he died for us" can be replaced by a more dynamic and three-dimensional explanation, "Jesus endured the worst the devil could do to him on the cross and died to restore 上帝 Jōtei's honor. He conquered sin and death by rising from the grave and made a way for us to return to relationship with 上帝 Jōtei."

Standing the Test

A key difference between the original state of Adam and Jesus is that

Adam was innocent, without knowledge of good and evil. In contrast, Jesus was born fully divine and fully man. Jesus had all of the human needs, desires, pleasures, and pains that people normally experience. Yet, Jesus was also fully divine – having only given up his glory to become human (Phil. 2:6-7). He was born to a human mother without a human father, thereby bypassing the curse of sin and estrangement from 上帝 Jōtei which was passed from father to child through Adam.

Adam had known 上帝 Jōtei's best but was innocent and when Satan tempted him, he fell. Jesus knew His identity and understood good and evil, so a temptation to rebel while in the prime of life at 30 years old would have no appeal to Jesus' physical nature. Without the hindrance of sin, Jesus had to be physically in a place where Satan's suggestion to rely on his own power, position, and authority would have any true appeal. Whereas Adam rebelled when he was tested, Jesus remained loyal to 上帝 Jōtei, enduring a shameful, torturous death on the cross. He did this to answer Satan's honor challenge and rescue humanity from the power of death, which Satan controlled (Heb. 2:14-15).

Hebrews 9:11-10:12 elaborates on the significance of Jesus' death on the cross through the comparison of Yom Kippur and the Crucifixion. The highlights of this passage are presented below from the LEB translation, while rendering 'redemption' in its more appropriate form of purification, indicated in italic letters.

> 9:[11] But Christ has arrived as a high priest of the good things to come. Through the greater and more perfect tent not made by hands, that is, not of this creation, [12] by his own blood, he entered once for all into the most holy place, obtaining eternal *purification*.
>
> .... [23] Therefore it was necessary for the sketches of the things in heaven to be purified with these sacrifices (the bull and goat), but the heavenly things themselves to be purified with better sacrifices than these. [24] For Christ did not enter into a sanctuary made by hands, a mere copy of the true one, but into heaven itself, now to appear in the presence of God on our behalf ....[26] ... but now (Jesus) has appeared once at the end of the ages for the removal of sin by the sacrifice of himself.
>
> 10:[11] And every priest stands every day serving and offering the same sacrifices many times, which are never able to take away sins. [12] But this one after he had offered one sacrifice for sins for all time, sat down at the right

hand of God.

This language of 'taking away sins' is also seen in Isaiah 53:6, "The Lord has laid upon him the iniquity of us all", :10 "an offering for sin", :11 "bear their iniquities", and :12 "he bore the sins of many". The parallelism in Leviticus 16:22 and Isaiah 53 is striking when one keeps the original Hebrew term of עָוֹן *ayon* instead of the various English renderings into guilt and iniquity.

The intent of drawing a comparison between the Suffering Servant of Isaiah 53 and live goat which was 'like Azazel' is obvious. Although Leviticus 16:22 says that the live goat will "carry away their iniquities" it has already been noted that this is a synecdoche which includes חַטָּאת *chata* and עָוֹן *ayon* within it. This helps tie into the typology of Hebrews 9 and 10 which sees Jesus as the High Priest, the slain goat, and the live goat all at once.

The only sticking point is Isaiah 53:5, which in translation gives a prescriptive rendering that "he was pierced because of our transgressions, crushed because of our iniquities." The rest of this prophecy is descriptive of who the Suffering Servant would be, yet this verse alone is rendered prescriptively. It would be more contextually appropriate to render it, "he was pierced through our transgressions, he was crushed by our iniquities." This is in keeping with Judas' transgression of betrayal, and the Sanhedrin's twisting of their authority as Israel's religious leaders. This is yet another example of shameful cultural eisegesis to fit the prevailing later Roman cultural understanding of salvation.

CHAPTER 22: SALVATION TRIAD

The final use of the Shame Triad is in explaining how salvation works for us. Since we defined sin through the Triad as Greed, Shame, Fear, and Strife, the Salvation Triad should demonstrate the antithesis to these traits. Like the Shame Triad, this offers a visual story of our new identity when we submit our lives to Jesus as Lord and Savior. Passively, we are cleansed by Jesus, while the Salvation Triad is meant to demonstrate our active participation.

For the core of the Salvation Triad, the opposite of greed is generosity, or giving. There is a kanji, 報い *mukui*, that means reward and by Chinese design appears to be a man laying his hands 𠂇 on an offering 又, illustrated on the left as a man or God 土, over a lamb 羊.[1]

Of course, this is of Chinese design, so we need to be able to answer if the Chinese ever practiced animal sacrifice in the worship of 上帝 ShangDi. The answer is yes, but the exact nature and form of these sacrifices is beyond the scope of this book.[2] At the twice-yearly border sacrifices, the Emperor of China would present multiple gifts, including a bull, which could also be represented by the 羊 *yáng* symbol in Chinese.

As demonstrated in chapter 19 the Japanese practiced different forms of blood sacrifice as well as offering various other gifts during お祓い Oharai for the cleansing of their hearts and land from 罪 *tsumi* and 穢れ *kegare*. Although such offerings are no longer practiced in Japan, it is still relevant to

---

[1] Timothy Boyle, *The Gospel Hidden in Chinese Characters* (Xulon Press, 2015), 146.

[2] Ethel R. Nelson, et. el., *God's Promises to the Chinese* (Read Books Publisher, 1997), 88. "The sacrificial death of Jesus had been represented by thousands of burning bulls offered by successive emperors of China at the annual Border Sacrifice."
See also Timothy Boyle, *The Gospel Hidden in Chinese Characters*, 15-16, 146.

Shintō: the Gospel's Gate

the culture and history.

We can introduce 報い *mukui* through the story of Abraham sacrificing Isaac in Genesis 22:9-13. In summary, Abraham had reached out his hand toward Isaac, tied upon the altar, when 上帝 Jōtei called out, and Abraham saw the ram caught in a bush behind him. This is not to argue that the 漢字 kanji is designed from this story, simply that it can be used to illustrate the story.

The portion on the right can be explained as depicting Abraham with his hands on his son, tied to the alter. The portion on the left showing the ram provided by 上帝 Jōtei.

In the spring of 2018, I helped facilitate an eight-week evangelistic Bible study to a group of Chinese college students, about four of the nine Chinese in attendance were seekers. I introduced 報い *mukui* to represent offering of the lamb that God provided in place of Isaac. The response from all of the Chinese present (including the Christians) was surprise, but also an almost immediate connection to the story. I also used this 漢字 kanji during the study of Passover and Yom Kippur.

After two weeks of using 報い *mukui*, I asked them what Bible story was represented by 報 and they were all able to recall at least one of the stories and one seeker was able to share the sacrifice of Isaac, Passover, and Yom Kippur.

Surprisingly, the seekers all anticipated that this was pointing toward Jesus. This established, to my mind, the typological value of 報い *mukui*, in conjunction with the typological stories of the Bible where it is most natural to introduce it.

All this is to explain why I have decided to use 報い *mukui* as the center of the Salvation Triad. When we come to Jesus, we lay our hands upon the Lamb of God, trusting in Him to cleanse us from sin and rescue us from death.

On the motivation side of the Salvation triad, the center is 報い *mukui*, the three petals represent what we give to 上帝 Jōtei. In the top, we give our 穢れ *kegare*, our impurity, the source of our shame, so that Azazel can carry it away.

In the bottom left there is the kanji for worship 祭, which is also part of 祭

Shintō: the Gospel's Gate

り matsuri. This is fitting since part of worship is a celebration of who 上帝 Jōtei is and what He has done for us. The bottom right petal is 忠 *chyū* loyalty. This kanji demonstrates that we are loyal to what is in the center of our heart.

On the stative side of the Salvation Triad, representing our new identity, the core is peace, the topmost petal is represented by honor, the bottom left by authority, and the bottom right by security. We have peace in our hearts because it is through Jesus that we receive honor, authority, and security in life.

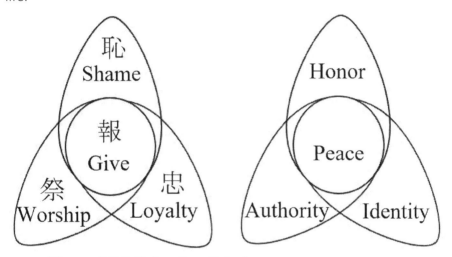

Figure 22.1 Salvation Triad

While the stative side of the Salvation Triad is something that we receive when we become Christians, it is also something that we must actively cultivate. Our experience of honor, authority, and security grow through the spiritual disciplines and an understanding of our new identity. This provides a visual means to help the Japanese and others conceptualize what the new life of being a Christian is about.

Burdens

In a more pragmatic application, the role of Jesus as Azazel, the God Who Carries Away, is the invitation to place our burdens upon Christ. For many Japanese, there is an explicit rule not to cause trouble or be a burden for others. However, 1 Peter 5:7 invites us to place our burdens upon him. There is no qualifier in the verse to restrict the burdens we place upon Him. Whether that burden is a crushing weight such as depression, a daily burden such as homework, or anything in between, Scripture tells us to place them upon Jesus "because he cares for you."

Showing weakness and asking for help is a sign of weakness and shame for many Western men and most Japanese. Yet, for Jesus, carrying those burdens and helping us in our weakness is a source of pleasure. The motivation is not duty or long-suffering but as an expression of 上帝 Jōtei's care for us, his beloved creation.

A parallel verse to 1 Peter 5:7 is Philippians 4:13, "I can do all things through him who strengthens me." This phrase, "I can do" is a poor translation when considered with the preceding verses. Paul is speaking of being in times of plenty and times of being in want. Human experience shows that having plenty (or having excess) can be just as burdensome as being in want. Yet Paul says that he has found the secret to dealing with both circumstances. It is Christ who gives him strength to endure these two extremes.

Though the average Japanese may not deal with hunger, the pressure of success for businesspeople and musicians sometimes leads such people to self-harm. Jesus stands ready to help them endure the pressures that they face. Loneliness and isolation are constant problems for many people in the age of the internet, regardless of their nationality. Jesus stands ready to help them endure and lead them out of the desert.

While in the rite of Yom Kippur, the goat carries away the iniquity and impurity of Israel, the NT authors also demonstrate Jesus, as Azazel, is able to carry the hardships of life (Phil. 4:13, 1 Peter 5:7). This is done willingly and not with an air of burden or frustration. This is something that Jesus wants to do for all people, if they will let him.

Deliverance Ministry

The petal of authority is about our spiritual authority, replacing the fear of spirits. Just as Jesus had authority over demons, illness, and death, Christians are called to use this authority – but authority must be studied, exercised, and cultivated. This is dealing with deliverance ministry – the breaking of curses and the expelling of demons.

A Christianity without this is a neutered Christianity that fails to follow two-thirds of the great commission (Luke 9:1, Mark 16:15-18), as Paul wrote, "my speech and my preaching were not with the persuasiveness of wisdom, but in demonstration of the Spirit and power" (1 Cor. 2:4, LEB). Mark 16:15-18 is sometimes considered an added passage and discounted. However, Mark can be diagramed in a pyramid fashion, which links the opening of Mark to the closing of Mark. This is a literary form that was used by both Greek and Hebrew writers.

Without these closing passages, the pyramid structure collapses. The number of verses in each "step" varies, but the verses were added by Drunk Munk Gutenberg who did not understand literary units. (See Ephesians 5:26-6:9 which is a thematic list of Superior to Inferior commands, and yet split into two chapters. There are many more examples where the writer's message is spliced because of Gutenberg's chapter and verse insertions.) Secondly, literary units do correlate to sentences.

It is natural for Jesus to tell his disciples to go out and cast out demons, heal the sick, and proclaim the Gospel because this is exactly what he told them when he sent them out in small groups previously. Casting out demons was a signature element of Jesus' ministry and is later used as a proof of the uniqueness of the Gospel when the Seven Sons of Sceva are beaten naked by a possessed man.

Outside the United States and Europe, deliverance ministry is an essential part of Christian Ministry. In the West, demons are often content to avoid attention and align with the Enlightenment worldview. Throughout the Gospels and Acts there are countless stories of people being set free from demonic oppression and torment.

An unbalanced view in the European Middle Ages that all mental and physical illnesses were caused by demons does not discount the fact that the Bible deals with demons as true threats that Christians are equipped to expel. Just as the hypochondriac does not disprove the need for hand washing, so the misuse and over-interest in demonic abilities does not discredit the demonic role in this visible world.

In Japan, this is a reality that must be faced. The history and nature of

Shintō: the Gospel's Gate

Shintō as a form of geomancy, necromancy, and mediums, with the ancestral practice of human sacrifice, and the fact that going to the Shintō shrine involves inviting the kami into the practitioner's body, means that there is an urgent need for the church to address the demonic harassment, oppression, and torment of Christians. Just as the Israelites had to drive out the Philistines, Canaanites, and others from the promised land, we need to expel the demons that have attached themselves to people prior to and after becoming Christians.

This is a subject that suffers from a lack of equipping in the Church. A solid foundation of deliverance ministry guidelines is beyond this book. A short list of recommendations is: Spirit of the Rainforest by Mark Andrew Ritchie; Out of the Devil's Cauldron by John Ramirez; The Word Came with Power by Joanne Shetler; Bondage Breaker by Neil T. Anderson, They Shall Expel Demons by Derek Prince, and Gods of Power by Philip M. Steyne.

I feel however, that a few guidelines are essential.

1) We operate under umbrellas of authority and cannot expel demons where we have not been invited to do so. In some locations deliverance ministry without consent is considered assault.

2) Never ask a demon for its name. 99.9% of the time, Jesus did not discuss anything with a demon. The Gadarene demoniac is the only recorded instance and there is a very specific set of circumstances which led to the question. Mark 5:1-13 and Luke 8:26-33 are not prescriptive examples.

3) If there are questions, ask the people present and the Holy Spirit, never interview a demon.

4) Do not accuse, argue with, challenge, or insult a demon. 2 Peter 2:10b-12, and Jude 8-10 instruct us not to slander spirits and warn that there are some people who have died because they have done so. Such actions may open a foothold for the demonic to attack the deliverance minister.

5) Stand in your position and authority of Jesus. "Papa, help me!" is a prayer that invites the Holy Spirit to manifest on our behalf. Confess personal and ancestral involvement with witchcraft, sexual sins, and other areas that are relevant to the person. Then break the demonic foothold, then expel the demon, and then ask the Holy Spirit to replace the demonic foothold with a foothold of righteousness.

Chapter 23. Conclusion

Western Christianity was introduced to Japan in mid-16th century and almost immediately took an adversarial stance toward Shintō. There are entire books written about how Shintō is the source of Japanese resistance to the Gospel.

It has been the position of this author and this book that Shintō is in fact an important ally to explaining the Gospel to the Japanese. Shintō's emphasis on cleansing and returning to the creative path is not contrary to the Gospel. Shintō is in search of the final 贖物 agamono, just as the Levitical system was in search of the true Azazel.

Respecting Japanese culture and asking questions about the what, how, and why, has revealed two major redemptive analogies: お祓い Oharai and the Kōnomiya Jinja Hadaka Matsuri. It is my hope that by understanding Shintō and the Levitical system better, the Church will be better equipped to understand and explain the Gospel to Japanese and other shame-based cultures.

I expect that reexamining the Gospel through the frame of Yom Kippur and the Japanese perspective will revitalize the Western Church. Instead of being locked into a late Roman understanding of guilt-innocence, the Gospel can be viewed in terms of cleansing and honor-shame. Western culture has forever changed and the way we express the Gospel needs to change to meet the new cultural value system.

The Gospel must be understood as Genesis frames the crisis of Scripture. Satan separated mankind from 上帝 Jōtei by accusing Him of being untrustworthy. Jesus answered that challenge by living a perfect life and giving himself as a ransom on the Cross. When we become Christ followers, we are given honor, authority, and purpose through our relationship with the God-Man, the 神男 Shinotoko.

Shintō: the Gospel's Gate

Appendix 1: Beyond Japan

There are areas of application that arise which are outside Japan. Already mentioned is the opportunity to use this redemptive analogy for the Jewish people of today. Yom Kippur remains an important holiday to observant Jews around the world. They are taught that Azazel is a demon, but the ability to show that Azazel is actually a typological prophecy of Messiah Yeshua should have an incredible impact on the way the Gospel is presented and the attitude of many Hebrews toward the Gospel.

A second area of impact will be within Muslim contexts. As with the Jews, they are taught that Azazel is a demon, and being able to demonstrate Jesus through Yom Kippur should have a large impact. Additionally, the explanation of the Gospel as cleansing, rather than satisfaction of wrath, should have more appeal to the heart and mind of the culture. Presenting the Gospel as an honor challenge will also have more appeal and fit closer with the logic of Muslim culture.

A third area of impact is in within localized spiritual traditions and practices, otherwise called folk religion, since they usually do not have the systematization or wide-spread influence of Buddhism, Christianity, Hinduism, Islam, Judaism, Shintō, or Taoism. This does not minimize the importance of these spiritual practices – they may even be more important to the practitioner since they are part of what sets the group apart from the outside world and helps establish identity. There are two examples to present from this category.

The first example comes from Nigeria.

> There was the Edi festival, of ritual cleansing whereby a symbolic fire brand was made and lighted torches waved over adherents' heads to ward off all their human miseries and death. They would also pray the divinities to grant them long life similar to Christian concept of eternity in union with God.

Shintō: the Gospel's Gate

> The cleansing ritual is crowned on the seventh day by a human scapegoat called Tele (similar to the biblical scape-goat at atonement: Lev.16:20-22), through which the sins of the inhabitants were carried away by means of a type of life-for-life substitutionary sacrifice. Tele was usually an Ife slave. He was offered to bear the people's sins, misfortunes, diseases and death into the traditional grove."[1]

During my time in China in the fall of 2017 I met Dr. Lekan Adebayo, who is from Nigeria. I asked him about these scapegoat rituals, and he was familiar with them. Dr. Adebayo said that they still take place in parts of Nigeria, mostly in the south, and the human scapegoat is usually killed. It is part of traditional religious practices to appease the spirits. He agreed that using Yom Kippur and the scapegoat as a redemptive analogy would be a way to help reach the people who are practicing such rituals today.

The second example comes from the United States. I spoke with Tony Shaw who is from the Lakota Nation of Native Americans. We were discussing Shintō: the Gospel's Gate and he told me about the Sun Dance ritual. It is a three-day rite and the central element is that a man volunteers to take the impurities of the community upon himself. This volunteer is always a man. He is purified for three days by fasting and being in the sweat lodge. After his purification, wearing just a loincloth, he is brought to a cottonwood tree.

This cottonwood tree has had all limbs trimmed so it is just the trunk. The man has hooks pierced through his breasts, and then leather cords are strung from the hooks to a tree. He leans back so that the cords are pulled tighter and tighter until the hooks are ripped out of his skin. By suffering on behalf of the community, the group is cleansed from their impurity and bad luck for the coming year.

I suspect, that further questioning of Lakota practitioners would reveal that the impurity of the community is passing through the volunteer, up the ropes, and into the tree. It is the tree itself that ultimately absorbs the impurity, but it is only through the conduit of a man, willing to endure great suffering on the community's behalf, that this transfer can take place.

---

[1] Gabriel Oyedele Abe, "Redemption, Reconciliation, Propitiation: Salvation terms in an African Milieu," *Journal of Theology for Southern Africa* 95, (July 1996): 3-12. ATLA Religion Database with ATLASerials, EBSCOhost (accessed August 22, 2016), 7.

Shintō: the Gospel's Gate

There are other questions that could be explored and answered with further interviews and observation: Why is it called the Sun Dance? Why is the volunteer pierced through the breasts and not the biceps or back? Was the person who is pierced always a volunteer? Did the Sun Dance involve human or animal sacrifice in the past? Is there a special name for this volunteer who suffers for the community? Why is it a man who suffers and not a woman? Is there a specific age of the volunteer? What time of year does this ritual take place? Is there significance to this chronology? Are there any songs, art, or performances connected with this ritual? What are other rituals that deal with purity, renewal, harvest, birth, or death in the Lakota spiritual system? These are just a few of the questions that deserve to be explored and answered.

The Lakota Sun Dance and the person who is pierced belong to what I would call a modified scapegoat ritual. Modified because there is no spatial movement of the person who takes away the impurity, curses, or bad luck of the community. We would be very well served to pay attention to things in cultures that have the feature of removing some form of negative spiritual elements from the community.

The fourth and final example is another modified scapegoat ritual, though it is not tied to any particular culture. Yet it helps show the universal application of this motif, even in such rationalistic cultures as the United States.

Dr. Al McKechnie taught Ministry Care at Columbia International University for many years. I took his Ministry of Counseling course in the spring of 2014. He related to the class that occasionally he would have a client who was stuck emotionally or spiritually in a past sin or trauma event. When it was appropriate, he asked the client to write down the story of the event on a piece of paper. Either as a confession of guilt or a confession of the trauma, and the suffering that it was causing them.

When the client had written the event down, Dr. McKechnie would join with him or her in prayer, lifting up the contents of the letter, sometimes even placing their hands on the paper. Then he would, as a representative of Christ, forgive the client and affirm that the sin has been taken away and they stand innocent before God. Once this was done, Dr. McKechnie would put the paper into a shredder, thereby removing the sin or trauma event from the client ritually. He said that this use of ritual in counseling often had a profound impact on the client – and most of his counseling career has been among Americans.

Although Dr. McKechnie referred to this as 'ritual in counseling', he never – to my memory – described it as a scapegoat ritual. However, the mechanics are identical. An individual places their impurity (caused by self or other) onto the recipient (the piece of paper), then an official (the counselor) joins in the confession as a representative, and sends the impurity away – in this case by destruction.

In e-mail correspondence, Dr. McKechnie elaborated,

> We have used shredding in several of the classes since a cognitive assent to Christ's death on our behalf does not seem to be enough for people to let go of their sin and shame and shift it to the cross. I am a firm believer in experiencing through the senses what it is that we need to believe and understand about Christ. Writing the sins down, placing them in the shredder and hearing the unique sound of the list being shredded helps the brain experience cognitive truths. Most of the rituals of the OT and NT involve water, clothing, the body, tastes and smells.[2]

This is a unique application of the concept of carrying away sin to cleanse the heart demonstrated in the Gospel. Special note is due that Dr. McKechnie says that the ritual "helps the brain experience cognitive truths." The rituals help the person experience the truth emotionally, whereas theological statements remain in the cognitive realm alone.

Perhaps the only modification needed to use Dr. McKechnie's ritual of shredding is that the terms used should change for guilt-innocence and shame-honor cultures. For American's, Dr. McKechnie pronounces the client forgiven before God. However, people from shame-based cultures would be more keyed to the word cleansed. The reality is the same between both statements, but the perspective of the client changes.

It is my hope that this very brief survey of scapegoat rituals in other cultures will help the Church identify similar areas of opportunity to explain the Gospel to those seeking a way to be cleansed from their impurities and rescued from the fear of death.

---

[2] Al McKechnie, personal e-mail correspondence, December 26, 2018.

APPENDIX 2: IDENTIFYING SHAME

In Appendix 2, I have attached a booklet titled Shame Drama: the Fall, which was originally published in 2013 through the Smashwords.com e-book self-publishing website. It has been edited for readability and the skit itself can be found in appendix 3.

There are a few reasons to attach this to Shintō: the Gospel's Gate. First, it is where I first put down on paper my wrestling with and understanding of shame and guilt. Secondly, the skit is a powerful evangelistic tool to get people interested in hearing the Gospel. And third, upon reflection, this is where I started developing the Shame Triad, although it was not yet conceived of in such a written form.

The reader will note that I have maintained the incorrect use of 罪 *tusmi* as guilt. Also, I use shame, fear, and alienation in this paper, instead of altering them to shame, fear, and strife. This is because I think it is important that the reader can see the development of my thinking in the triad.

Introduction

In the summer of 2012, I joined a small group from Christar, led by Chuck Burwell, traveling to Japan for a three-week mission trip. My preparation for the trip included examining different ways of communicating the Gospel to the Japanese that were effective. Chuck said that drama had been well received, so I set about writing a skit attempting to give an answer to the question "What went wrong?"

I considered using Abraham, Jesus, or the Demoniac, but they all needed background. It was during this process that a lecture from the class, Introduction to the Gospels, in the spring of 2011 came to my mind. Professor Don N. Howell, Jr., who has fifteen years of experience as a missionary in Japan and is a professor of New Testament and Greek at

Shintō: the Gospel's Gate

Columbia International University, mentioned that it is important when ministering with the Japanese to lay the foundation of Creation from the Biblical account since the Buddhist and Shintō creation stories are vastly different. Accordingly, the setting of the Garden of Eden became an obvious choice.

Three Characters

One of the problems that had to be reconciled was the presence of Eve. When the Genesis account opens, it shows broad brush-strokes of the creation event in chapters 1-2, but then goes back to day six and focuses on the creation of man (much like a movie which pans over a city before going back and focusing on a particular street). This is a chronological shift which seems to be missed by many Western readers. With this in mind, the account shows God giving the command regarding the fruit of the tree of the Knowledge of Good and Evil to Adam before Eve was created (Gen. 2:16-22).

This, then shows that Eve was not given the command not to eat of the Tree of the Knowledge of Good and Evil. It was a restriction placed on Adam. Presumably, instructing Eve regarding this command was part of his role as a leader. Unfortunately, when Satan came to tempt Eve in Genesis 3:3, she added to the Lord's command "do not touch," which provided a foothold for Satan's accusation against the Lord. After she ate the fruit, Gen. 3:6 says, "she also gave some to her husband, who was with her, and he ate."

Adam's act of eating the forbidden fruit is his third failure: Adam taught the command to Eve incorrectly; He failed to take dominion over the Serpent and protect Eve; He ate from the tree that had been forbidden him.

It is also important to note that Eve's eyes were not opened until after Adam ate, hinting again that the command was given to Adam and it was his actions which were being tested. It is a common enough idea that the Fall was Eve's fault, but close attention to the chronology of events shows that the fault lays squarely on Adam's shoulders.

The decision to not include Eve has three main components: 1) How does one show Eve being created from Adam's rib? 2) Eve's inclusion distracts that the command was given to Adam, and it was Adam's act which brought about the curse of sin. 3) The inclusion of Eve would likely sidetrack the audience from the central crisis, namely: "Where did we come from?" "What went wrong?" and, "Is there hope?"

Coincidently, this limitation gives the skit an emphasis on the number three; three characters; three actions – creation, innocence, fall; three kanji; and an implied three stages of mankind – innocent, fallen, and redeemed.

After about a month of writing and discussion with Chuck Burwell, the end result was a ten-minute skit about the fall of man in the Garden of Eden, which I titled The Shame Drama. We were able to perform the skit twice in Ube, and once in Columbia, SC (for a group of mostly Chinese graduate students). Each time, the skit was very well received and resulted in much discussion. However, to my frustration a good portion of that discussion were questions revolving around the use of 罪 tsumi for guilt.

Identifying Shame

Reading the account of the fall repeatedly, the most striking difference in the before and after is that Adam and Eve had no shame before they ate the forbidden fruit, but then immediately felt shame and made coverings for themselves afterward. Yet this idea of shame was something I had not previously explored, nor could I remember any substantive teaching about what shame was.

There has been a large amount written about the substance and value of shame, so a brief definition will suffice here. Sam Louie explains, "Shame communicates the message that we're weak, defective, dirty, and worthless."[1]

From the psychological perspective, Andrew Morrison writes, "Shame is fundamentally a feeling of loathing against ourselves, a hateful vision of ourselves through our own eyes . . . . shame generates concealment and hiding, and the wish for acceptance (by self or other)."[2]

Muller traces the Biblical foundation and finds that, "All through the Bible, references are made to shame and honor in various forms . . . .. In all there

---

[1] Sam Louie, *Asian Shame and Addiction: Suffering in Silence* (Create Space, 2013), 49.

[2] Andrew Morrison, *Culture of Shame* (Northvale: Jason Aronson Inc., 1998), 13, 14.

are more than 190 references to honor in the Bible . . . . The bible also addresses shame, mentioning it over one hundred times."³

He continues,

> Shame generally follows any action perceived by the larger group to reduce one's standing or status within the group . . . . Shame leaves us with a sense of humiliation, defeat, and ridicule and is intricately tied to our exposure and loss of honor or status before our peers and those in authority within our social network. Shame is . . . corporate and public; it cannot be experienced apart from the larger social context.⁴

Similarly, Tennent writes,

> The Old Testament contains at least ten different words . . . to convey various aspects of shame. These words include "to shame"; "scorn, insult, reproach, or disgrace"; "to publicly humiliate/afflict."⁵

Examining Guilt

Coming from a guilt-based culture, it is quite baffling when people from shame-based cultures cannot understand the concept of guilt. However, the opposite statement is sure to be true, with those from shame-based cultures baffled at the Westerner's inability to grasp the concept and importance of shame. Shame and guilt are such an intrinsic part of their respective worldview that these concepts are often unexamined and assumed, almost operating at the level of a self-evident truth.

Muller writes, "We in the west have taken the guilt theme and have traced it through the Bible. We have formed our understanding of the gospel and our systematic theology around this theme . . . . This is the standard western way of explaining the Gospel."⁶

---

³ Roland Muller, *Honor and Shame: Unlocking the Door* (Xlibris, 2000), 57.

⁴ ibid., 129.

⁵ Timothy Tennent, *Theology in the Context of World Christianity* (Grand Rapids: Zondervan, 2007), 134.

⁶ Roland Muller, *Honor and Shame: Unlocking the Door*, 100.

Shintō: the Gospel's Gate

Piers and Singer identify guilt "as a behavioral transgression of authoritative boundaries and the attendant fear of punishment."[7] Timothy Tennent offers a vital insight when he writes, "guilt arises from some *internalized* value system."[8]

If guilt arises from violating an internalized value system, then the value system that a guilt-based theology employs must already exist in the target group for it to communicate effectively to them.

To restate the problem, although the Gospel is translated into a native language, if the hope of the Gospel is not explained in terms of the culture's heart value, we may as well still be speaking in a foreign tongue. When attempting to reach people or cultures that do not share our internalized value system, or do not place the same emphasis on the priority of guilt, a guilt-based theology and evangelistic message becomes a hindrance to the communication of the Gospel.

To underscore the importance of the distinction, Bruce Nicholls writes,

> 'Shame' representing at least 10 different Hebrew roots and 7 Greek roots occurs nearly 300 times in the Old Testament and 45 times in the New Testament. 'Guilt' and its various derivatives occur 145 times in the Old Testament and 10 times in the New Testament."[9]

Clearly, the concept of shame is more important to the biblical authors than guilt, with shame occurring twice as much as guilt in the Old Testament and more than four times as much in the New Testament.

What is at issue here is the Western priority of teaching guilt before the Gospel can be understood. To draw a parallel, should the evangelist insist that an illiterate person or people group learn to read before sharing the Gospel? Or is it more appropriate for the evangelist to learn how to share the Gospel in a verbal format that the target group can learn, recite, and

---

[7] G. Piers and M. Singer, *Shame and Guilt: A Psychoanalytic and Cultural Study* (New York: Horton, 1953), quoted in Timothy Laniak *Shame and Honor in the Book of Esther*, (Society of Biblical Literature, 1998), 24.

[8] Timothy Tennent, *Theology in the Context of World Christianity*, 129. Emphasis mine.

[9] Bruce Nichols, "The Role of Shame and Guilt in a Theology of Cross-Cultural Mission," *Evangelical Review of Theology* 25, no. 3, 2001, 235-236.

understand – leading to faith – and then work on teaching the people how to read? This is exactly the process that is happening with Chronological Bible Storying[10] and other techniques being utilized to reach preliterate people groups.

In the same way, what is being suggested here is not an abandoning of the teaching on guilt, but simply sidestepping it at the outset, leaving the possibility of returning to it later. First reach the shame-based culture where their felt and true needs exist, and as their understanding of God's moral law develops, their understanding of their personal transgression of His law – their understanding of personal guilt – will also develop.

Bruce Nichols expresses this sentiment, "The proclamation of the gospel across cultural barriers must first address the issue of shame before it can effectively respond to the conscious or sub-conscious awareness of guilt..."[11] However, if that understanding of guilt never becomes an intrinsic aspect of their self-identity, it is no real loss, just as a previously illiterate people may never truly have a sense of ownership of written language.

Naming the Third Consequence

It was an encouragement to see the three groups engaged and asking questions about the events in the skit. However, it was discouraging that so much of that conversation revolved around the issue of guilt, 罪 *tsumi*.

It is a normal human reaction to say that the other is the problem in a situation. But, as Christians, we have a responsibility to follow Christ's example to speak in language and illustrations that the people we are ministering to will understand. An honest evaluation of the effectiveness of guilt as one of the consequences of sin found the term to be wanting.

Among the questions that came to mind during this time of reflection was, 'how can guilt be seen in the consequences of Adam's sin?' What internalized value system did Adam have? The laws did not exist yet, only the

---

[10] Grant Lovejoy, Chronological Bible Storying: Description, Rational, and Implications (Southwestern Baptist Theological Seminary, 2000).

[11] Bruce Nichols, "The Role of Shame and Guilt in a Theology of Cross-Cultural Mission," 237.

one law – Do not eat of the Tree of the Knowledge of Good and Evil – had been given, meaning that an internalized system also did not yet exist.

Shame could be seen in Adam and Eve making coverings for themselves out of fig leaves. Fear could be seen with them hiding from God when they heard Him walking in the Garden. The third consequence, if not guilt, needed to be something emotional or visible, in keeping with the nature of the first two consequences.

Reading the action again, consciously not labeling anything as guilt, the third consequence seemed to be Adam and Eve's exile 遠 *en* from the Garden of Eden.[12] Yet exile is an action term which does not reflect the changed condition of the heart. The exile of Adam and Eve from the Garden of Eden is the most noticeable consequence of Adam's rebellion; however, it is an external consequence.

Before he is exiled from the Garden, Adam's relationship with God has already been broken. Since one of the Shame Drama's goals is to examine the heart consequence of Adam's rebellion, what was needed was a term to reflect the change in relationship between Adam and God.

During a conversation with Professor Don N. Howell, Jr. in November of 2012, I spoke to him of the difficulty in naming the condition of exile, and his immediate suggestion was alienation. 疎外 *sogai* means estrangement, neglect, alienation, or casting out depending on its usage.[13] Paul gives a picture to this separation as being a prisoner to the law of sin in Romans 7:23.

With the three consequences of sin in mind, the Gospel forms a chiasm with the account of the Fall. Dr. Howell writes that Luke's account of Satan's temptation of Jesus (4:1-13) parallels the temptation of Adam and Eve appealing to physical needs, power, and independence.[14] Jesus endures the

---

[12] C. H. Kang and Nelson, Ethel R., *The Discovery of Genesis: How the Truths of Genesis Were Found Hidden in the Chinese Language* (Saint Louis: Concordia Publishing Group, 1979), 79.

[13] Jim Breen, WWWJDIC, http://www.csse.monash.edu.au/~jwb/cgi-bin/wwwjdic.cgi?1F Monash University, 2011. Last accessed 6/6/13.

[14] Don N. Howell, Jr. *The Passion of the Servant* (Eugene, Resource Publications, 2009), 32-33.

temptation that Adam fell to and proves himself righteous by remaining obedient to God's will, fulfilling God's purpose for his life.

Christ's identification is completed at the end of his ministry, when he endures the consequences of Adam's rebellion between his arrest and his death: Fear in the Garden of Gethsemane; Shame in being crucified; and Alienation when he cries out "My God, my God, why have you forsaken me?" in Matthew 27:46 and Mark 15:34.

Guilt is certainly not absent in the Crucifixion. Jesus was tried and condemned with murderers in the place of a rebel. Examining the Greek in Luke 23:14 shows Pilate identifying Jesus with the word ἀποστρέφω *apostrephō* which could be interpreted as rebellion or to incite rebellion.[15] This is reflected in the skit with God casting Adam from the Garden for rebelling against him.

Timothy Tennent wrote, "In Adam we became identified with guilt, fear, and shame. In Christ we are now identified with forgiveness, confidence, and honor."[16]

But in reflecting on the consequences of sin it seems more appropriate to say that in Christ we have honor, authority, and adoption. As it is written "the glory of children is their fathers" (Prov. 17:6), "for God gave us a spirit not of fear but of power" (2 Tim. 1:7), and "God sent forth his Son, born of a woman, born under the law, to redeem those under the law, that we might receive adoption as sons" (Gal 4:4-6).

Final Thoughts

The Shame Drama should be easy for any ministry with three people to perform, regardless of the language group. All that is necessary is for the characters on the sash to be re-written to the appropriate words in the target culture.

It is strategic that the characters are never addressed by name. I think that by leaving them nameless, it will be easier for the audience to personally

---

[15] Blue Letter Bible, http://www.blueletterbible.org/lang/lexicon/lexicon.cfm?Strongs=G654&t=NASB last accessed 6/13/13.

[16] Timothy Tennent, *Theology in the Context of World Christianity*, 150, 144.

identify with them. Furthermore, prejudices against the name of God, Adam, or Satan are not brought to the forefront of the mind.

One criticism that was offered for the skit early on was that it did not offer a resolution, leaving the audience in a state of anxiety regarding the fate of Adam. While this criticism is true there are a few reasons for the lack of resolution.

First, the biblical account of the Fall does not offer any resolution, and the story goes from bad to worse with Cain's murder of Abel.

Second, and more importantly, once resolution is given, the audience can stop thinking about the problem. It no longer has the emotional hook to keep them engaged. Since they will identify with Shame, Fear and Alienation in their own lives, they will wonder what can be done for them personally.

Shame is an evaluation of our self-worth, our ability to live up to expectations of ourselves from internal and external sources. Fear is our evaluation of ourselves to the outside environment. And alienation is the loss of emotional intimacy between self and other, especially the Creator in whose image man was created. The Shame Drama helps the audience recognize the presence of sin in their own hearts, which helps to open the door for sharing how Jesus identified with and overcame these consequences of sin.

Shintō: the Gospel's Gate

APPENDIX 3: SHAME DRAMA

Materials:

The stage should have a partition or a screen such as a doorway or a dry erase board that Satan can hide behind and look out from the corner.

A simple box wrapped or plain, easy to open, and large enough to hold the sash.

A sash which can be easily placed around Adam's shoulders with the kanji for shame 恥 haji, fear 恐 osore, and alienation 疎外 sogai written on it.

Two masks for Satan, one being a villain mask, the second being a hero mask which needs to be able to be held up or be worn to hide the villain mask.

Skit:

The scene opens with Adam lying motionless on the ground. God enters and pantomimes creating trees and animals. When he reaches Adam, he should kneel, keeping Adam between himself and the audience, and mimic piling dirt into a form, then lift Adam up by the shoulder until he is standing.

God: I, the Lord, I have created you, so you are my son. See, this is the work of my hands and I give you authority over it. But I have a special gift for you.

God takes the box and hands it to Adam. As God picks up the package, Satan looks out from his hiding place, wearing the villain mask.

God: There is something very precious inside this box. But you must not open it.

Adam: Thank you, father.

God walks off stage. Satan puts a hero mask over the villain mask and approaches Adam.

Satan: That is a lovely gift, but I know a secret.

Adam: A secret?

Satan: Yes. Your father knows what is in the box. And he does not want you to have it.

Adam: What could it be?

Satan: Go on, take a peek. No one will know. Your father wants to keep you a child forever. Be a man, open the box.

Adam opens the box and Satan pulls out the sash and puts it around Adam's shoulders. Adam looks at the scarf with a crestfallen expression.

Satan removes the hero mask and moves aggressively toward Adam. Adam cowers away.

Satan: Shame! Shame! Foolish boy!

God reenters stage and looks at Adam and Satan.

God: What have you done?

Adam falls to his knees, his face to the ground.

Adam: Lord (or Master), I – I . . .

God: Did you open the gift I commanded you not to?

Adam: This man came and he-he said that you were keeping something good from me, and I opened the box.

God: Because you have rebelled against me, you are no longer my son. You must leave and not return.

Adam hurries off the stage, covering his face.

God turns to Satan and points at him.

God: Because you have done this, one day I will restore him, but I will destroy you! Be gone!

Satan flees the stage. God walks off the stage. Skit ends. Allow silence for a minute or so, so the audience can soak in the skit.

Do not explain the skit for the audience.

Foreign Word Lexicon

Alphabetized by Transliteration
Phonetic rendering of Hebrew taken from L. A. Mitchel, *A Student's Vocabulary for Biblical Hebrew and Aramaic* (Grand Rapids: Zondervan, 1984)

Agamono 贖物 ransom

Amenominakanushi no Kami 天之御中主の神 God at the Glorious Center of Heaven, one of the three spirits of creation in the Kojiki

Aphesis ἄφεσις G859 translated as forgiveness in most English translations; KJV translates as remission or carry away

Azav עזב to remove, carry away, send into exile

Awon עָווֹן 'ā/wŏ́n twist

Azazel עֲזָאזֵל traditional translation as demon or scapegoat. Biblical interpretation is "God who removes (our sin and impurity)."

Amenominakanushi no Kami 天之御中主の神 God at the Glorious Center of Heaven

Cohen כֹּהֵן priest

Chyuu 忠 loyalty

El אֵל god, gods, common noun, parallel to spirit or mighty one, in line with the original Greek and Germanic understanding of the word god. Can be used to indicate YHWH in context.

El'elyon אֵל עֶלְיוֹן "God Most High" or "God Above All"

Shintō: the Gospel's Gate

Elohim elochey t'shu'ati אֱלֹהִים אֱלֹהֵי תְּשׁוּעָתִי Elohim, God of My Salvation (Ps. 51:14)

En 遠 exile

Ez עֵז ʻēz goat

Fundoshi 褌 a Japanese style loincloth, similar to what Sumo wrestlers wear

Hadaka Matsuri 裸祭り Naked Man Festival

Haji 恥 shame

Chata חָטָא ḥā/ṭā' to separate, sin; one of three terms for sin in Hebrew.

Chatath חַטָּאת ḥaṭ/ṭā't sin offering; purge

Hitobashira 人柱 a human sacrifice (=immolation)

Hitogaki (kanji unknown) human hedge; people buried alive in a circle around a grave. Perhaps 人垣.

Hitogata 人形 human shape paper doll for Oharai

Hitomigokuu 人身御供 human sacrifice

Hitomigokuuageru 人身御供上げる the act of human sacrifice

Jōtei or Shōtei 上帝 Emperor Above Heaven and Earth. Traces to the Tang Dynasty pronunciation of 上帝 ShangDi.

Jinja 神社 Shintō Shrine

Kabas כָּבַס kā/ḇás wash

Kabash כָּבַשׁ kabash to tread down; bring into bondage.

Kami 神 generally translated as god, but better understood as spirit.

Kamimusubi 神結び Spirit of Creation, one of three creator spirits in the Kojiki

Kami-Sama 神様 leader of the kami, a current word for God in the Japanese translations of the Bible. Also used to speak of customers by store employees.

Shintō: the Gospel's Gate

Kannushi 神主 Shintō Priest

Katashiro 形代 "form-substitute", human shaped paper doll for お祓い Oharai

Kebes כֶּבֶשׂ, keh-bes´ to dominate; a ram (just old enough to butt):—lamb, sheep.

Keves כֶּבֶשׂ or Kisev כֶּשֶׂב sheep

Kegare 穢れ impurity, stain, to draw blood. 怪我 was suggested by Dr. Boyle and is phonetically identical to 穢れ but are not used for their own meaning, "strange self".

Kippur כְּפוּר ki/pur cover, expiate; cleanse, purify, purification

Kuriŏs κύριος one in supreme authority: God, Lord, master.

Machah מָחָה mā/ḥâ' wipe away, blot out

Matsuri 祭り festival

Me 目 pronounced like "meh", Japanese for eye.

Melek מֶלֶךְ King or Emperor

Miqdash מִקְדָּשׁ Sanctuary or "place of holiness" from the root word קָדוֹשׁ qadosh

Miko 巫女 shrine maiden

Misogi 禊ぎ ritual acts of purification that may be performed any day

Mukui 報い to give, to reward, report.

Musubi 結び in Shintō creative energy; in general Japanese it means to tie knots

Nademono 撫物 "thing for rubbing", human shaped paper doll for Oharai

Oharai お祓い Great Purification ceremony held twice a year at most jinja

Osore 恐 fear

Ouranou kai ges kuriŏs οὐρανοῦ καὶ γῆς κύριος Lord of Heaven and Earth

Peshah פֶּשַׁע pé/šaʻ to trespass or transgress; to stray, one of three terms for sin in Hebrew

Shintō: the Gospel's Gate

Qadosh קָדוֹשׁ holy

Qariv קָרִיב offering

Racham רָחַם suggests a tender, maternal love such as a mother would have for her child

Salach סָלַח sā/láḥ forgive; remove, restore.

Seh שֶׂה śeh lamb

Seppuku 切腹 ritual suicide by disembowelment, women were allowed to slit their throats

ShangDi 上帝 Han Chinese pronunciation of the Creator God in China. Rendering into Japanese should be Shaddai.

Shaphat שָׁפַט Judgement, assessment, or evaluation.

Shi 死 death

Shinotoko 神男 'god man', the man chosen to bear the 罪 tsumi and 穢れ kegare of the community at the 裸祭り Hadaka Matsuri

Sogai 疎外 estrangement, neglect, alienation, or casting out

Taher טָהֵר ṭā/hḗr cleanse

Takamimusubi 高皇産霊神 High Spirit of Creation. One of three creator deities in the Kojiki

Tentei 天帝 Heavenly Emperor, an alternative rendering of 上帝 ShangDi in China

Toga 咎 or 科 1) (uk) error; mistake; fault; (2) (uk) sin; wrongdoing; offense

Tsumi 罪 sin, crime, to catch a contradiction. 罪 tsumi expresses the Shintō idea of twisting, straying, and becoming separated from the correct path. Parallel to the Hebrew words to twist, stray, and separate. The result of 罪 tsumi is 穢れ kegare.

Tsumibito 罪人 used in Japanese bible translations to mean sinner. In regular use, it means criminal.

Tsumihoroboshi 罪滅ぼし atonement for sins; amends; expiation; penance. 罪滅ぼしの expiatory. 罪滅ぼしため as an atonement for one's sin; in atonement for (=in expiation of) sins (=crimes)

Shintō: the Gospel's Gate

Tumah טֻמְאָה *ṭum/'â'* impurity, uncleanness; the result of sin in Hebrew thought.

Wa 和 harmony

Yang 羊 lamb, sheep, or goat, using the Han Yu 汉语 pronunciation.

Yomi 黄泉 Land of the Dead; Netherworld or Hades

Yūrei 幽霊 angry ghost

Zoukanosanshin 造化の三神 the three creator gods, may have the impression of three separate gods rather than the Christian doctrine of Trinity.

Shintō: the Gospel's Gate

WORKS CITED

Part 1: From the Garden to the Grave

Bianchi, F. D., Mangum, D. R., Brown, R. Klippenstein, & R. Hurst (Eds.), *Lexham Theological Wordbook:* Rebelliousness. Bellingham, WA: Lexham Press, 2014.

Blue Letter Bible, http://www.blueletterbible.org/index.cfm.

Boyd, James W. and Ron G. Williams. "Japanese Shintō: An Interpretation of Priestly Perspective." *Philosophy East & West* 55, no. 1 (Jan2005): p33-63. *Academic Search Premier,* EBSCO*host* (Accessed December 22-15).

Boyd, James W, and Ron G Williams. "Artful Means: An Aesthetic View of Shintō Purification Rituals." *Journal Of Ritual Studies* 13, no. 1 (1999 1999): 37-52. *ATLA Religion Database with ATLASerials*, EBSCO*host* (accessed March 2, 2016).

Breen, Jim. Wwwjdic.com. Monash University.

Eiki, Hoshino. *Kodansha Encyclopedia of Japan vol 4*. New York: Kodansha International, 1983.

Genchi, Katao. *Study of Shintō: the Religion of the Japanese Nation*. Tōkyō: The Zaidan-Hōjin-Meiji-Seitoku-Kinen-Gakkai, 1926.

Georges, Jason. . *In the Beginning . . . Honor*, http://honorshame.com/beginning-honor. 2014.

Geisler, Norman L. and William D. Watkins. *Worlds Apart: A Handbook on Worldviews; second edition*. Eugene: Wipf and Stock Publishers, 2003.

Hee, Kong. God in Ancient China. Singapore: Attributes Publishing, 2009. DVD.

Hiebert, Paul G. "The flaw of the excluded middle." *Missiology* 10, no. 1 (January 1982): 35-47. *ATLA Religion Database with ATLASerials*, EBSCO*host* (accessed March 24, 2016).

Jenni, E., & Westermann, C. *Theological lexicon of the Old Testament*. Peabody: Hendrickson Publishers, 1997.

Kang, C. H. and Ethel R. Nelson. *The Discovery of Genesis: How the Truths of Genesis Were Found Hidden in the Chinese Language*. St. Louis: Concordia Publishing House, 1979.

Kikawa, Daniel. "God's Fingerprints in Japan." Hawaii: Aloha Ke Akua Ministries, 2008. DVD.

Kato, Genchi. *Study of Shintō, the Religion of the Japanese Nation*. Tōkyō, Japan: Maruzen Company, Ltd. 1926.

Mason, J. W. T. *Meaning of Shintō*. New York: E. P. Dutton and Co. Inc, 1935.

Matthews, K. A. *Genesis 11:27–50:26 vol. 1B*. Nashville: Broadman & Holman Publishers,

2005.
Mitchel, L. A. *A Student's Vocabulary for Biblical Hebrew and Aramaic.* Grand Rapids, MI: Zondervan, 1984.
Ono, Sokyo. *Shintō: The Kami Way.* Rutland, Vermont: Charles E. Tuttle Company, 1962.
Pickens, Stuart D. B. *Historical Dictionaries of Religions, Philosophies, and Movemnts No. 38 Shintō.* Maryland: Scarecrow Press, 2002.
Piers, G. and M. Singer, *Shame and Guilt: A Psychoanalytic and Cultural Study.* New York: Horton, 1953.
Richardson, Don. *Eternity in Their Hearts,* 3rd Edition. Bethany House Publishers, 2008.
Sansom, George. *A History of Japan vol. 1.* Stanford: Stanford University Press. 1958.
Scrivener, F. H. A. *The New Testament in Greek* (Ac 17:24–25). Cambridge: Cambridge University Press. 1881.
Steyne, Philip M. *Gods of Power: A Study of the Beliefs and Practices of Animists.* Columbia: Impact International Foundation, 2005.
Strong, J. *A Concise Dictionary of the Words in the Greek Testament and The Hebrew Bible (Vol. 1).* Bellingham, WA: Logos Bible Software, 2009
Tennent, Timothy C. *Theology in the Context of World Christianity: how the global church is influencing the way we think about and discuss theology.* Grand Rapids: Zondervan, 2007.
Toyohiko, Kagawa. *Christ and Japan, 3rd printing.* New York: Friendship Press, 1934
Witthoff, D., Lyle, K. A., & Nerdhal, M. (2014). *Psalms Form and Structure.* (E. Evans, Ed.). Bellingham, WA: Faithlife.
Yasumaro, O. *Tales from Ancient Japan, or the Kojiki by Yaichiro Isobe.* Tokyo: San Koku Sha. 1929.

Part 2: From Death to Life

Abe, Gabriel Oyedele. "Redemption, Reconciliation, Propitiation: Salvation terms in an African Milieu." *Journal of Theology for Southern Africa* 95, (July 1996): 3-12. ATLA Religion Database with ATLASerials, EBSCOhost (accessed August 22, 2016)
Adu-Gyamfi, Yaw. "The Live Goat Ritual in Leviticus 16," *Scriptura* (Online) 112, (2013): 1-10, ATLA Religion Database with ATLASerials, EBSCOhost. Accessed August 22, 2016.
Anderson, Neil. *The Bondage Breaker.* Eugene: Harvest House Publishers, 1990.
Aston, W. G. *Shintō: The Way of the Gods.* New York: Longmans, Green, and Co., 1905. Project Gutenberg ebook.
Ayto, John. *Dictionary of Word Origins.* New York: Arcade Publishing, 1990.
Baker Encyclopedia of the Bible. Grand Rapids: Baker Book House, 1988.
Barker, K. L. *Micah, Nahum, Habakkuk, Zephaniah.* Nashville: Broadman & Holman Publishers, 1999.
Benedict, Ruth. *Chrysanthemum and the Sword.* Rutland: Charles E. Tuttle & Co., 1976.
Boyle, Timothy. *The Gospel Hidden in Chinese Characters.* Xulon Press, 2015.
Brand, C. and others, eds. *Holman Illustrated Bible Dictionary.* Nashville: Holman Bible

Publishers, 2003.

Chalke, Steven. "Redemption of the Cross," in *The Atonement Debate*, ed. Derek Tidball, David Hilborn, and Justin Thacker (Grand Rapids: Zondervan, 2009)

Cohen, Doron B. *The Japanese Translations of the Hebrew Bible: History, Inventory, and Analysis.* Boston: Brill Academic Publishers, Inc, 2013.

Corduan, Winfried. *Neighboring Faiths: a Christian Introduction to World Religions.* Downers Grove: Intervarsity Press, 1998

Cross, F. L. and E. A. Livingstone, editors. *The Oxford Dictionary of the Christian Church*, 3rd ed. rev. New York: Oxford University Press, 2005.

Cyril of Alexandria. *Letters of St. Cyril of Alexandria, volume 1.* Translator John I. McEnerney. Washington: Catholic University of America Press, 1987.

Davies, Nigel. *Human Sacrifice: In History and Today.* New York: Morrow, 1981.

Endo, Shusaku. *A Life of Jesus.* Translator Richard A. Schuchert. Ramsey: Paulist Press, 1973.

Fairbairn, Patrick. *Typology of Scripture, Two Volumes in One, b1.* Reprint; Grand Rapids: Kregel Publications, 1989.

Florenz, Karl and Ernest Mason Satow. *Ancient Japanese Rituals and the Revival of Pure Shintō.* Kegan Paul Japan Library (Unnumbered). New York: Columbia University Press, 2002. Accessed from University of Oregon Library 01-10-17.

Gane, Roy. *Cult and Character: Purification Offerings, Day of Atonement, and Theodicy.* Indiana: Eisnbrauns, 2005.

Genchi, Kato. A *Study of Shintō: the Religion of the Japanese Nation*. Tōkyō: The Zaidan-Hōjin-Meiji-Seitoku-Kinen-Gakkai, 1926.

------. *What is Shintō?* Tokyo: Maruzen Company Ltd., 1935.

Gulick, Sidney Lewis. *Evolution Of The Japanese, Social And Psychic.* New York: Fleming H. Revell Company, 1903.

Hearn, Lafcadio. *Japan: an Attempt at Interpretation.* A Public Domain Book, 1907.

Herbert, Jean. *Shintō: At the Fountain-head of Japan.* New York: Stein and Day Publishers, 1967.

Hiebert, Paul G. *Anthropological Insights for Missionaries.* Grand Rapids: Baker Book House, 1985.

Howell, Don N, Jr. *The Passion of the Servant: A Journey to the Cross.* Resource Publications: Eugene, 2009.

Jacobs, T. L. *Virtue and Vice Lists,* in The Lexham Bible Dictionary, ed. J. D. Barry, et al. Bellingham, WA: Lexham Press, 2016.

Jenni, E. and C. Westermann. *Theological Lexicon of the Old Testament.* Peabody: Hendrickson Publishers, 1997.

Judisch, Douglas. "Propitiation in the language and typology of the Old Testament." *Concordia Theological Quarterly* 48, no. 2-3. April 1984: 221-243. ATLA Religion Database with ATLASerials, EBSCOhost (accessed August 22, 2016.

Kagawa, Toyohiko. *Christ and Japan.* Translator William Axling. New York: Friendship Press, 1934.

Katsumata, Senkichiro. *Kenkyusha's New Japanese-English Dictionary: An Entirely New*

Edition. Tokyo: Kenkyusha Limited, 1954. Previous editions 1918 and 1951.

Lee, Samuel. *Rediscovering Japan, Reintroducing Christendom: Two Thousand Years of Christian History in Japan.* New York: Hamilton Books, 2010.

Marsh, Herbert. *Lectures on the Criticism and Interpretation of the Bible.* London: J. Smith Printer to the University, 1828.

McQuilkin, Robertson. *Understanding and Applying the Bible: Revised and Expanded.* Chicago: Moody Press, 2009.

Milgrom, Joseph. *Leviticus 1-16: A New Translation with Introduction and Commentary.* Doubleday: New York, 1991.

Mitchel, L. A. A Student's Vocabulary for Biblical Hebrew and Aramaic. Grand Rapids, MI: Zondervan, 1984.

Nagmag, Nagoya's Magazine. Konomiya Hadaka Matsuri. http://nagmag.jp/konomiya-hadaka-matsuri-february-28-2018. Posted May 25, 2018. Last accessed May 25, 2018.

Nelson, Ethel R. and C. H. Kang. *The Discovery of Genesis: How the Truths of Genesis Were Found Hidden in the Chinese Language.* St. Louis: Concordia Publishing House, 1979.

Nelson, John K. *A Year in the Life of a Shintō Shrine.* Seattle: University of Washington Press, 1996.

Orr, J., J. L. Nuelsen, E. Y. Mullins, and M. O. Evans, editors. *The International Standard Bible Encyclopedia, vol. 1–5.* Chicago: The Howard-Severance Company, 1915

Peters, Ted. "Atonement and the Final Scapegoat," *Perspectives In Religious Studies* 19, no. 2 (1992). ATLA Religion Database with ATLASerials, EBSCOhost (accessed August 22, 2016).

Pinker, Aron. "A Goat to go to Azazel." The Journal of Hebrew Scriptures vol. 7, 2007. Accessed 1-16-18, http://www.jhsonline.org/Articles/article_69.pdf.

Plutschow, Herbert. *Festivals of Japan.* Surrey: Japan Library, 1996.

Ramm, Bernard. *Protestant Biblical Interpretation: A Textbook of Hermeneutics*, 3rd rev. edition. Grand Rapids: Baker Books House, 1970.

Roberts, Alexander and James Donaldson, editors. *Ante-Nicene Fathers, Volume 3, Latin Christianity: Its Founder, Tertullian. I. Apologetic; II. Anti-Marcion; III, Ethical.* Hendrickson Publishers, 2004.

Robinson, Greg. "Sidney Gulick." Densho Encyclopedia. Accessed 04-13-19. https://encyclopedia.densho.org/Sidney%20Gulick/.

Russell, J. H. "Expiation, Propitiation" in C. Brand, and others, eds., *Holman Illustrated Bible Dictionary.* Nashville: Holman Bible Publishers, 2003.

Smeaton, George. *The Doctrine of the Atonement According to the Apostles* (Winona Lake: Alpha Publications, 1979.

Strong, J. *A Concise Dictionary of the Words in the Greek Testament and The Hebrew Bible* vol. 2. Bellingham, WA: Logos Bible Software, 2009.

Tambasco, Anthony. *A Theology of Atonement and Paul's Vision of Christianity.* Collegeville: Liturgical Press, 1991.

Tennent, Timothy C. *Theology in the Context of World Christianity: how the global church is influencing the way we think about and discuss theology.* Grand Rapids: Zondervan,

2007

Tidball, Derek, David Hilborn, and Justin Thacker, editors. *The Atonement Debate*. Grand Rapids: Zondervan, 2009.

Tsuda, Noritake. "Human Sacrifices in Japan," *The Open Court* vol. 1918, issue 12, Article 6, (12, 1918). http://opensiuc.lib.siu.edu/ocj/vol1918/iss12/6.

Turnbull, Stephen, *Samurai – the World of the Warrior*. Osprey Publishing, Limited, Oxford, 2003.

Walvoord, J. F. and R. B. Zuck. *The Bible Knowledge Commentary: An Exposition of the Scriptures Vol. 2*. Wheaton: Victor Books, 1985.

Wu, Jackson. "The Yin-Yang of Contextualization," Patheos. Posted 8-23-16, http://www.patheos.com/blogs/ jacksonwu/2016/08/23/the-yin-yang-of-contextualization/

Yamaguchi, H. S. K. *We Japanese*. Yokohama: Yamagata Press, 1937; reprint, Yokohama: Yamagata Press, 1950.

Appendixes

Abe, Gabriel Oyedele. "Redemption, Reconciliation, Propitiation: Salvation terms in an African Milieu," Journal of Theology for Southern Africa 95, (July 1996): 3-12. ATLA Religion Database with ATLASerials, EBSCOhost. Accessed August 22, 2016.

Howell, Don N. Jr. *The Passion of the Servant*. Eugene, Resource Publications, 2009.

Laniak, Timothy. *Shame and Honor in the Book of Esther*. Society of Biblical Literature, 1998.

Louie, Sam. *Asian Shame and Addiction: Suffering in Silence*. Create Space, 2013.

Lovejoy, Grant. *Chronological Bible Storying: Description, Rationale, and Implications*. Southwestern Baptist Theological Seminary, 2000.

Morrison, Andrew. *Culture of Shame*. Northvale: Jason Aronson Inc., 1998.

Muller, Roland. *Honor and Shame: Unlocking the Door*. Xlibris, 2000.

Nelson, Ethel R. and Kang, C. H. *The Discovery of Genesis: How the Truths of Genesis Were Found Hidden in the Chinese Language*. Saint Louis: Concordia Publishing Group, 1979.

Nichols, Bruce. "The Role of Shame and Guilt in a Theology of Cross-Cultural Mission." *Evangelical Review of Theology* 25, no. 3, 2001.

Tennent, Timothy C. *Theology in the Context of World Christianity: how the global church is influencing the way we think about and discuss theology*. Grand Rapids: Zondervan, 2007

Shintō: the Gospel's Gate

WORKS CONSULTED

61-214-1-PB. "Live Goat Ritual." *Accessed through ATLA Religion Database with ATLASerials,* EBSCO*host*.

Amaladoss, Michael. *The Asian Jesus.* New York: Orbis Books, 2006.

Arai, Jin. "Religious Education in Christ with Culture from a Japanese Perspective." *Religious Education.* Vol. 91, no. 2 (Spring 1996): 222 Academic Search Premiere, EBSCOhost (accessed February 17, 2016).

Calvin, Parker F. *Christ in a Kimono: Christian Beliefs in Japanese Dress.* Kearney, NE: Morris Publishing, 1998.

Carmichael, Calum M. "The Origin of the Scapegoat Ritual." *Vetus Testamentum* 50, no. 2 (2000 2000): 167-182. *ATLA Religion Database with ATLASerials*, EBSCO*host* (accessed August 22, 2016).

Carter, John D. *Integration of Psychology and Theology.* Grand Rapids: Zondervan Corporation, 1979.

Chow, Alexander. "The East Asian Rediscovery of 'Sin'." *Studies in World Christianity 19, no. 2.* August 2013: 126-140. Academic Search Premier, EBSCOhost (accessed February 17, 2016).

Doerner, David L. "Comparative analysis of life after death in Folk Shintō and Christianity." *Japanese Journal Of Religious Studies* 4, no. 2-3 (September 1977): 151-182. *ATLA Religion Database with ATLASerials*, EBSCO*host* (accessed November 12, 2015).

Feinberg, Charles Lee. "The Scapegoat of Leviticus Sixteen." *Bibliotheca Sacra* 115, no. 460 (October 1958): 320-333. *ATLA Religion Database with ATLASerials*, EBSCO*host* (accessed August 22, 2016).

Georges, Jason. *3D Gospel: Ministry in Guilt, Shame, and Fear Cultures.* Timē Press, 2014.

Gilchrest, Eric J. "For the wages of sin is... banishment: An unexplored substitutionary motif in Leviticus 16 and the ritual of the scapegoat." *The Evangelical Quarterly* 85, no. 1 (January 2013): 36-51. *ATLA Religion Database with ATLASerials*, EBSCO*host* (accessed August 22, 2016).

Grabbe, Lester E. "The scapegoat tradition: a study in early Jewish interpretation." *Journal For The Study Of Judaism In The Persian, Hellenistic And Roman Period* 18, no. 2 (December 1987): 152-167. *ATLA Religion Database with ATLASerials*, EBSCO*host* (accessed August 22, 2016).

Gulick, Sidney L. *Evolution Of The Japanese, Social And Psychic.* New York: Fleming H. Revell

Company, 1903. Project Gutenberg Kindle Edition, 2004.

Hastings, Thomas John. "Protestantism's Perduring Preoccupation with Western Theological Texts." *Theology Today* 62 (2005): 49-57. *ATLA Religion Database with ATLASerials,* EBSCO*host* (accessed December 28, 2015).

Heim, S. Mark. "Visible victim: Christ's death to end sacrifice." *The Christian Century* 118, no. 9 (March 14, 2001): 19-23. *ATLA Religion Database with ATLASerials*, EBSCO*host* (accessed August 22, 2016).

Heiser, Michael S. *Unseen Realm*. Bellingham: Lexham Press, 2015.

Holtom, D. C. *The National Faith of Japan: A Study in Modern Shintō*. New York: Paragon Book Reprint Corp, 1965.

Hooke, Samuel Henry. "Theory and Practice of Substitution." *Vetus Testamentum* 2, no. 1 (January 1952): 1-17. *ATLA Religion Database with ATLASerials*, EBSCO*host* (accessed August 22, 2016).

Iwai, Shuma. "Japanese Christianity in the Meiji Era: An Analysis of Ebina Danjo's Perspective on Shintōistic Christianity." *Transformation (02653788)* 25, no. 4 (October 2008): 195-204. *Academic Search Alumni Edition*, EBSCO*host* (accessed November 12, 2015).

Janowitz, Naomi. "Inventing the scapegoat: theories of sacrifice and ritual." *Journal Of Ritual Studies* 25, no. 1 (2011 2011): 15-24. *ATLA Religion Database with ATLASerials*, EBSCO*host* (accessed August 22, 2016).

Japan Illustrated Encyclopedia Vol. 1. New York: Kodansha America, 1993.

Jensen, C. B. and A. Blok. "Techno-animism in Japan: Shintō Cosmograms, Actor-network Theory, and the Enabling Powers of Non-human Agencies." *Theory, Culture & Society*, 30(2), 84-115. 2013.

Kennard, Douglass. "Jesus as Sacrifice." Houston Graduate School of Theology. Posted June 2011. Accessed 8-23-16. http://www.hgst.edu/wp-content/uploads/2011/06/Jesus-as-Sacrifice.pdf

Kenney, Elizabeth. "Shintō Funerals in the Edo Period." *Japanese Journal Of Religious Studies* 27, no. 3-4 (September 2000): 239-271. *ATLA Religion Database with ATLASerials*, EBSCO*host* (accessed August 25, 2016).

Kitamori, Kazo. *Theology of the Pain of God*. Translated from *Kami No Itami No Shingaku*. 5th Revised Edition. Tokyo, Japan: Shinkyo Shuppansha., 1958.

Kiuchi, Nobuyoshi. "Living like the Azazel-goat in Romans 12:1B." *Tyndale Bulletin* 57, no. 2 (2006): 251-261. *ATLA Religion Database with ATLASerials*, EBSCO*host* (accessed August 22, 2016).

Komuro, Naoko. "Christianity and ancestor worship in Japan." *Studies In World Christianity* 9, no. 1 (2003 2003): 60-68. ATLA Religion Database with ATLASerials, EBSCOhost (accessed November 12, 2015).

Kurtz, Johann H. *Sacrificial Worship of the Old Testament*. Translated by James Martin. Edinburgh: T & T. Clark, 1863. Accessed on January 4, 2018 at https://books.google.com/books?id=y0BOAQAAMAAJ&source=gbs_navlinks_s

Lee, Samuel. *Understanding Japan Through the Eyes of Christian Faith*. Amsterdam: Foundation University Press, 2015.

--------. *The Japanese and Christianity*. Amsterdam: Foundation University Press, 2014.

Manser, M. H. *Dictionary of Bible Themes: The Accessible and Comprehensive Tool for Topical Studies*. London: Martin Manser, 2009.

Mann, Allen. "Western Shame." http://honorshame.com/the-gospel-for-western-shame. Accessed 12-9-15.

Mullins, M. R. "What About the Ancestors? Some Japanese Christian Responses to Protestant Individualism." *Studies In World Christianity*, 4(1), 1998.

Nelson, Ethel R., Richard E. Broadberry, Ginger Tong Chock. *God's Promises to the Chinese*. TN: Read Books Publisher, 1997

OMF. *A Christian's Pocket Guide to the Japanese*. Ross-shire, Scotland: Christian Focus Publications, 2008.

Ramirez, John. Out of the Devil's Cauldron.

Richie, Mark Andrew. Spirit of the Rainforest. Island Lake: Island Lake Press, 2000.

Sadler, A W. "The Grammar of a Rite in Shintō." *Asian Folklore Studies* 35, no. 2 (1976 1976): 17-27. *ATLA Religion Database with ATLASerials,* EBSCO*host* (accessed August 25, 2016).

Shillington, V George. "Atonement Texture in 1 Corinthians 5.5." *Journal For The Study Of The New Testament* 71, (September 1998): 29-50. *ATLA Religion Database with ATLASerials*, EBSCO*host* (accessed August 22, 2016).

Tsuda, Noritake. "Exorcism and Sardines Heads (Illustrated)." *The Open Court*. Vol. 1917, issue 9, Article 6, (September, 1917): 563-9.
https://opensiuc.lib.siu.edu/ocj/vol1917/iss9/6. Last accessed 07-17-2018.

Weaver, J. Denny. *Nonviolent Atonement*. Grand Rapids: Eerdmans, 2001.

Westbrook, Raymond and Theodore J Lewis. "Who led the scapegoat in Leviticus 16:21?" *Journal Of Biblical Literature* 127, no. 3 (September 2008): 417-422. *ATLA Religion Database with ATLASerials*, EBSCO*host* (accessed August 22, 2016).

Wu, Jackson. "Seeking God's Face: Honor and Shame in the Sacrificial System." *Jackson Wu. Doing Theology. Thinking Mission.* Posted December 03, 2015. Accessed May 12, 2018. http://www.patheos.com/blogs/jacksonwu/2015/12/03/my-ets-papers/

--------. *4 Keys to Evangelism in Honor-Shame Cultures*. Jackson Wu. Doing Theology. Thinking Mission. May 13, 2015. Accessed December 10, 2015. http://www.patheos.com/blogs/jacksonwu/2015/05/13/4-keys-to-evangelism-in-honor-shame-cultures/Accessed 12/10/15

--------. *John 3:16 is Not the Gospel*. Patheos.com, 2015.

INDEX OF FIGURES AND TABLES

Figure 1.1	Honor Challenge	7
Figure 2.1	Origin and Progression	20
Figure 2.2	Shintō Levels	22
Figure 4.1	Missing Categories	26
Figure 8.1	Shame Triad	53
Figure 8.2	Effects of Kegare	54
Figure 10.1	Increased Honor	62
Figure 10.2	Earned Honor	62
Figure 16.1	Agamono	107
Figure 19.1	Lamb	142
Figure 20.1	Culture Drum	144
Figure 21.1	Honor Triad	154
Figure 22.1	Salvation Triad	161
Table 1.1	Isaiah 14	11
Table 5.1	Types of Tsumi	34
Table 6.1	Psalm 51	38
Table 6.2	Honorifics	39
Table 7.1	Ritual Impurity	48
Table 8.1	Story of Tsumi	52
Table 12.1	Updated Psalm 51	75
Table 13.1	Kippur Flow Chart	79
Table 14.1	Hileos	88
Table 19.1	Types and Antitype	137

About the Author

Brian T. McGregor earned his bachelor's degree in interpersonal and cultural communication from the University of South Florida and his Master of Divinity from Columbia International University.

Brian has been studying the Japanese language and culture for fifteen years with an eye toward moving to Japan, where he hopes to see the emergence of an ethnic church.

While at Columbia International University, Brian served in intercultural ministries, including one targeting discipleship and evangelism of Japanese.

Shintō: the Gospel's Gate

Shintō: the Gospel's Gate

cci

Made in United States
Orlando, FL
08 February 2022